TRENT'S WALK
WITH AN ANGEL

Aunt Rosie!
I hope you enjoy our grandson Trent's story. He's now 5½ years old and still exemplifying glorious strength in fulfilling his God given Mission on earth. You two have that in common.
I pray yourself well. God Bless.
Love
Dawn Lew-Estes

Trent's Walk With An Angel

*An Inspiring Journey
Of God's Design
For All Humankind*

DAVID W. ESTES

Trent's Walk With an Angel. Copyright © 2014 by David W. Estes. All rights reserved. Printed in the United States of America. No part of this book may be used or reproduced in any manner whatsoever without written permission from the author, except in the case of brief quotations embodied in critical articles or reviews. For information or permissions, address David W. Estes at P. O. Box 170664, Arlington, TX 76003.

ISBN: 1506013988
ISBN-13: 9781506013985
Library of Congress Control Number: 2015900154
CreateSpace Independent Publishing Platform,
North Charleston, South Carolina

10 9 8 7 6 5 4 3 2

FOREWORD

I was inspired to write this book as a gift to Trenton's mommy, daddy, his siblings and his Aunt Bec. I wanted to immortalize this little man's life story for them and for posterity. As his story evolved, I realized that his life has implications far beyond a single family unit and this humble tribute. His is the story of a great man in a little dysfunctional body. One without the ability to communicate, who sends a clear message to all who witness him. One who endures relentless daily pain for the pleasure of a loving bond between himself and his family. One without sight who can open others' eyes to see their personal disappointments, failures, pains, and perceived suffering as a mere bump in life's road. One who blesses the faithful with soul-searching, prayerful pondering. One who is a true living instrument of God to make doubters deliberate and think. One who emanates love and courage with each breath. One who lives with the angels.

> David Estes
> Kennedale, Texas
> April 20, 2014

ACKNOWLEDGMENTS

I first and foremost thank my Lord for allowing me to pen His revealing story of our beloved Trent. I truly believe the words within this book are His and I was merely the conveying instrument. I thank my loving wife Pat for her lifelong support of my endeavors. I give recognition and heart-felt gratitude to Trent's great-aunt Chris Cowan for taking my unpolished draft and lovingly transforming it into a clear and proper book. Finally, I thank my loving daughter Nicki and son-in-law Shane for trusting me with their beloved Trent's story.

Trent's Walk with an Angel

1

THE JOURNEY BEGINS

In the essence of my life, I am floating in a warm, blanket-like, fluid environment. I can feel and hear a profound rhythmic pounding that appears to be above and outside my environment. This awareness has been with me from the beginning. Coinciding with my beginning was a miraculous event: for a brief time I was not alone. A spiritual being of some sort appeared and said it was a messenger from God. The angel embraced me, and its touch gave me a feeling of comfort and connection.

It spoke to me in a muffled language-noise I sometimes hear coming from far beyond my environment. It said, "You are a child of God, conceived in his image, with an eternal soul." It told me, "God loves you and always will love you and has chosen you to serve a special purpose in life." It explained that I am to lead an extremely challenging, painful, and short life. God's intent, it assured me, is not to punish me; to the contrary, God's will is that I survive and bring a message to all who meet me. It said that I will have many imperfections and various physical limitations, but that my birth and my very existence will lead others to humility and to soul-searching, prayerful thought, and they shall ask God for his blessing and their salvation. It said I will be loved by all who witness me.

When my work is finished, it continued, I will rise to the kingdom and glory of heaven. Then I will be healthy and whole, free from human pain and suffering. And one day I would be reunited with my family in God's presence. It said that in the meantime I would live the special heavenly purpose God has for me. Suddenly the angel was gone. I didn't understand much of what he said, but some words stuck with me. "Love" and "God" comforted me especially. Soon I drifted off to sleep.

I wake to muffled language-noises outside my environment. I wish I could understand the noises. They are not all the same; the loudest is more constant and seemingly the closest. Others are higher pitched, and some are low. Many other non-language-noises come and go. It appears to me, though, that it's a lot noisier and more confusing outside than it is in my environment.

I sleep a lot. Besides the noises that occasionally wake me up, my environment sometimes is unsettled and moves around, keeping me awake. I don't understand why the movement occurs; at times it rolls or it bounces

The Journey Begins

or it shakes, and I roll or bounce or shake along with it. Now it's quiet and still, and I sleep.

After many awakenings I discover that I have limbs growing on me, and I wonder what they are for. I also discover I have a small rhythmic pounding inside me. It's much quieter than the rhythmic pounding noise outside my environment. I listen to more muffled language-noise until I fall asleep.

Suddenly I awake to a lot of loud noises unlike anything I've heard before; it shakes me and my environment. The rhythmic pounding noise that has always been near me is pounding faster. The new bursting noise is different and frightening. At times it whistles, bangs, booms and crackles, over and over again. I think it will never stop. It becomes even louder and turns into a faster, thunderous roar. Just as suddenly it stops! Then I only hear lots of language-noise, but it's happy and reveling. The rhythmic pounding noise is slower now, as it was before.

Later I hear a rhythmic language-noise that I've never heard before. A lot of language-noise is forming a repeated message that says words like "happy" and "birth" something and the words "Sto lat." The rhythmic pounding noise speeds up a little, and I hear a long whoooooshing sound from somewhere very close to my environment, then more happy language-noise sounds. The bursting and booming noises frightened me earlier, but this new rhythmic language is soothing. I soon fall asleep.

I am noticing that my environment is getting smaller. My limbs have grown fingers and toes on their ends. Sometimes I kick my legs and feel some force from outside my environment pushing down and moving over the area I kicked. I wonder what that is.

Many naps later the angel appears and says, "You are almost to term." I look blankly at the spirit, and it chuckles and says, "That means soon you will leave your environment." I ask, "Where will I go?" He responds, "To LIFE. Not to worry, though, for I will be your guide, your angel. Now you must sleep and gain strength."

When I awake, I find myself upside down. What is happening? Some force from outside is pushing down and moving over me a lot. I feel my head pressed against the bottom of my environment. My hand somehow finds its way to my mouth and I fall back to sleep for a while.

Suddenly the warm liquid blanket in my environment disappears. I'm being forced lower and lower. The loud rhythmic pounding noise outside of me is fading, and I feel pressure all around me, squeezing me tighter and tighter. The rhythmic pounding noise inside me beats louder and faster. I think something is pulling at me, and I feel a chill for the very first time. My angel reveals itself and in a gentle reassuring voice says, "Today is your birthday."

The Journey Begins

Something slides under me and lifts me away from what was my warm environment. I am still cold. I am rolled over and feel an object, connected to something called a Doctor-Kim-voice, poking in and out of my mouth and my nose, drawing the last fluids of my environment from me. When the doctor-voice's hand aggressively pats my back, I instinctively draw my first breath, then gag and cough. I try to cry out but make no sound, hear no noise. I sense a dark, foggy, dim light prying into my eyes. It is a different kind of darkness, unlike the black comfort of my environment. I shake, I tremble, I attempt to cry out again, but I hear nothing. I am so, so cold.

My angel embraces me, which brings warmth and calm. I tell it sadly, "I miss my environment." Something called a nurse-voice then moves me and lays me down on a hard surface. The nurse-voice proceeds to poke, turn, push, twist, and pull me. I next feel something being wrapped around me; it is warm and dry. I am moved again and cradled against something soft and warm. Then a gentle voice says, "Hello, Trent. I'm Mommy. I love you." The only word I can understand is "love," and that comforts me. I can hear other language-voices. The Daddy-voice says, "I love you, Trent." The Doctor-Kim-voice says, "You're beautiful, Trent."

A little later, I hear a nurse-voice say, "He needs to spend a few hours in the NIC-U [Neonatal Intensive Care Unit] for observation." The Mommy-voice kisses me and says, "I love you and will see you soon." The nurse-voice moves me to a less comfortable surface that the Daddy-voice begins to push somewhere else.

On the way my angel reappears and tells me the NIC-U nurses will bathe me and then place me in a glass-enclosed bed under a special light to improve my color. They will also monitor my "vital statistics." The angel says it will stay with me. I understand only that it will stay with me.

As we continue down the corridor, we encounter many language-voices that the Daddy-voice stops next to and says, "It's a boy. His name is Trenton, but we'll call him Trent." The many language-voices revel in the news and in the name *Trent*. My angel explains, "That's you. Your name is Trent. The revelers are your family members: your brother Tyler, sisters Triny and Tori, and your cousins, aunts, uncles, and grandparents. They love you and are excited to see you on your birthday." Then I realize the Mommy- and Daddy-voices are family, too.

We arrive at the NIC-U, and another nurse-voice places me on a hard surface. My warm wrap is removed, and again some nurse-voices begin poking, pulling, twisting, tapping, and turning me from side to side. They put things in and out of every opening in my body. I am cold. They move me and put a warm fluid on me, rubbing it all over and around me. They rub harder and rougher, and I am shaking from the cold. They put more liquid on me. I'm afraid and wonder, "Why can't I cry? Don't they know I'm cold?" Again more liquid is poured on me, only this liquid is warmer, much warmer. They finally stop and dry me off and rewrap me. My angel embraces me in the warmth of its pure light. Then they move me to the clear glass bed with a light over it that my angel told me about. I am warm and fall asleep.

I awake as the nurse-voice pushes my clear glass box into a room with other voices in it. She then cradles me against something familiarly soft and warm, and I hear a soft voice say, "Welcome back, Trent. It's Mommy. I love you." Another voice says, "Hi, Trent. It's Daddy. I love you, too." Then other much louder and irregular voices bellow out, "We love you, Trent!" Mommy says, "That's your brother Tyler and your sisters Triny and Tori, who are also your family." I'm so thankful for my family!

After a nice rest, I am gently awakened by my Mommy-voice, who says, "It's time for your feeding." I don't understand the words. The Mommy-voice tries and tries to get me to nurse, but I just can't understand what to do. I keep hearing the word "latching," but I just can't figure out what that is and how I am supposed to do it. Eventually the nurse-voice tells my Mommy-voice she will have to pump her milk and feed me by bottle. The 80ml bottle feedings work but not well and are difficult for my Mommy-voice. It takes over an hour to feed me the 80mls, and I always spit a lot up. The feedings are repeated every two and a half hours, so my Mommy-voice doesn't get much sleep, but she doesn't seem to mind. As I drift off to sleep, I hear her speak her favorite words: "I love you, Trent."

My angel enters my dream and tells me that I will awake to a new day and be examined by some medical staff, but he will be with me the whole time. I wake up to my Mommy-voice encouraging me to feed from my bottle. It takes longer than usual, and I spit up more than usual. My Daddy-voice takes me from my Mommy-voice's arms and raises me over his shoulder to burp me. He walks around while patting my back and speaking words I don't understand. Of course, I spit up on him; I can't seem to keep the milk inside me. Soon a nurse-voice comes and takes me to be examined.

The doctor-voices again poke, pat, pull, twist, and turn me. They put things in all my body openings and take x-rays. I hear words like "floppy head" and "vision disorder" and "core muscle disorder" and "reflex." When the doctor-voice says those words to my Mommy- and Daddy-voices, I hear them cry. At that moment I learn words can be painful, too.

A few feedings and naps later, I hear a doctor-voice explain to my Mommy- and Daddy-voices that I will be transferred tomorrow to Cook Children's Hospital in Fort Worth. Earlier, other voices said I would be going home, so perhaps Cook Children's is my home. I feel lonely and afraid during the ambulance ride there. My angel appears and explains it is against the rules for my Mommy-voice to ride with me, but she will meet me at Cook Children's. He speaks with a kind and soothing voice: "You will see there is no need to fear. I will be here with you." I thank God for my Mommy-voice and my angel.

I must have fallen asleep along the way because we are at Cook Children's when I awake. The ambulance-voices take me to a room where my Mommy- and Daddy-voices are waiting. My brother and sisters are there, too, so we all are able to spend a short time together. Daddy-voice tells brother- and sister-voices that I will be at Cook's for a few weeks or more. He explains to them that children visitors aren't allowed in the NIC-U where I'll be staying and urges them to kiss me and say their good-byes before the nurse comes to take me there. Their kisses were all over my face, making me wet and happy, and their good-byes were loud.

My angel remains with me continuously, and I notice that there are other angels here at Cook's. When I mention that, my angel tells me it is common practice for angels to appear in great numbers at any crisis center. I tell him, "I don't understand." He explains, "A crisis to an angel is when a being of earth is in terminal danger. Hospital intensive care units and emergency rooms are two of the most common crisis centers. The angels gather there to give prayerful thought and spiritual support and guidance to the patients. In many instances, an angel is a patient's conduit to God." I think I understand.

I feel like I have been at Cook Children's a long, long time. My Mommy-voice has been here with me most of the time. My Daddy-voice comes late in the day and helps feed and change me. The doctor-voices here do a lot of what they call "tests." I don't like the tests; they hurt a lot. The doctor- and nurse-voices put things in and out of my body's holes and, worse yet, through my skin. I learn to cry here. I wonder if this is the pain my angel told me about back at my beginning.

It is hard to sleep here. My angel explains that I am in a ward, or large room, along with about eighteen other newly born babies. Each of us has a separate area with enough room for the glass box we sleep in, monitoring instruments, life-support equipment, and a chair for Mommy- and Daddy- voices to share. Each machine makes some noise, and, of course, babies are crying pretty constantly. The time between feedings is short, so sleep time is short for me and for the Mommy-voice. Each time I return from tests, my Mommy-voice is here and puts her face close to mine, kisses me, and tells me she loves me. I learn the meaning of the word "love" from her.

Over time, other voices visit me. The Aunt Bec-voice comes to see me often and brings gifts for me and my glass box. My angel tells me that she also watches my brother- and sister-voices a few days a week so Mommy can go to work. He says, "Aunt Bec will be an important part of your life," and that comforts me. The MiMi- and Pop Pop-voices visit often, as do the Bapcia- and Dzia Dzia-voices. Each holds me, talks sweetly to me, and tries to feed me. Other voices also come to visit; sometimes I sleep and miss them.

Then one day the tests at Cook Children's Hospital are complete, and the doctor-voices schedule a meeting with my Mommy- and Daddy-voices. My Mommy's voice cracks when she tells me that she loves me before going to the meeting. I wish I could tell her, "I love you, too."

The doctor-voices schedule additional tests at the Cook's outpatient clinic in Dallas. They say they did what testing they could here, but the tests didn't provide answers to what is causing my disabilities. They say the specialists at the clinic will analyze my condition more fully. They also want to install a feed button on my tummy, explaining that it will be hooked up to a pump to drip feed me through the night, increasing my nutrition intake, reducing spitting up, and allowing me to sleep better at night. This procedure will be done in a month or so. "In the meantime," they say, "we're releasing Trent, and you may take him home." I can tell that my Mommy- and Daddy-voices' eyes are welling with tears.

2

LOOKING FOR ANSWERS

When the Mommy- and Daddy-voices return from the meeting, my Mommy-voice picks me up from the glass box and puts her face close to mine. She kisses me and says in a soft, happy voice, "*You* are coming home with Mommy and Daddy today." As my Mommy-voice presses her face close to mine again, I feel drops of warm liquid on her cheek.

I don't understand much of what she is saying, but the words "mommy," "daddy," and "love" I do, because they fill me with a warm, safe, happy feeling. I am a little confused, though; I thought Cook's was my home. Then I feel relief that I am leaving the place that taught me how to cry. I wonder if my angel knows where my home is. I hope he does.

Recently I have discovered I can tell my Mommy- and Daddy-voices from other voice-noise. It helps me to know that they are near. Mommy says, "Before we can go, Trent, I need to feed you and get you all dressed." I only understand "feed." I would like to tell her, "I'll try hard, Mommy," but I don't know how to say the words. The doctor-voice tells Mommy to increase my feedings to keep me within my growth percentile. I don't think I'm going to like that "percentile" word. The doctor-voice doesn't understand how much my food hurts me.

Later that day, after Daddy moves me into a chair of some kind with straps and buckles and puts it on a cart, a nurse-voice starts pushing it a long, long way. I can hear Mommy's and Daddy's voices, so I know they're coming, too. When the cart stops, Mommy leans down, kisses me, and tells me, "Just a little while more, my sweet boy, while Daddy goes to get the car." Then Daddy is back, picks up my chair, and sets it in whatever Mommy calls it—I can't tell what it is—and places even more straps over the chair. When we finally start to move, the steady motion soothes me to sleep.

While I am sleeping, my angel comes to me in a dream. He says, "I am just hitching a ride." I don't understand what that means, but I'm happy he's with me. When we arrive at the place they call "home," Daddy gently carries me inside while I continue to sleep.

I finally awake to a lot of voice-noise. Mommy picks me up while kissing me and saying, "Welcome home, Trent! We have company. First, you'll eat, and then you'll meet and mingle with everyone for a short time." After my feeding and, of course, spitting up in front of everyone, Mommy announces, "It's time for pictures of you with the family." All the other voices seem to gather close around Mommy and me. They each repeatedly say, "Welcome home." One thing is very clear: I am *really* home.

Next, I am passed into the arms of the other voices for the thing my mommy calls "pictures." Each one is told to say, "cheese," and after it does, another voice says, "Wait, wait. Let me take one, too!" It says "cheese" again and sometimes again. First, I am placed in the arms of my brother and sisters. They are louder than I recall from back on that first day at Cook's. Now loud is all they speak, and I hear them clearly over the others today. The brother Tyler puts his face close to mine. I think he is going to kiss me like Mommy does, but instead he yells, "Booo! Booo! Booo! Booo! Booo!," frightening me. Then sister Trinity shoves a stuffed turtle toward my face, tells me its name, and adds that she loves some little ponies, too. The sister Tori comes up to me, kisses my cheek with a loud smacking noise, and runs off. I don't understand what they say, but I sure can hear them.

I hear a soft voice I recognize, Aunt Bec, who gently lifts me from Mommy, saying, "Come here, big boy," and chuckling a little. She cradles me in her arms, kisses me, rubs her nose against mine, and tells me, "You are so beautiful. I love you and will always be here for you."

She takes me aside and sits rocking me for a time. Then she says, "It's Bapcia's turn to hold you!" Bapcia's touch is so familiar; when she cradles me against her chest, I sink in and feel secure. She kisses me, pats my back, and checks my diaper all at the same time. She's good!

Bapcia croons in my ear, "I can't wait to take you home with me and care for you, just you and me." Then I hear a loud, rough voice say, "What about me?" I don't understand the language he speaks, and it sort of frightens me. Mommy says, "Don't be afraid, Trent. It's just Dzia Dzia trying to sound like Donald Duck." I don't get what that means. I am a little nervous as Bapcia places me in his arms. When he brings me close to his lips and gently whistles in my ear, I recognize him. He does that a lot! When he's holding me and talking to me, I feel it down to my bones. Mommy soon says, "Trent's had a busy day and needs to nap now." I understand that word "nap," and it pleases me.

Over time many more voices come to my home to hold me and say words I don't understand. I recently discovered that there are other, very different voices moving around in the house. They don't use the same language-voice I'm used to. Instead they use a woof-woof and a cryyy language-noise. I think Triny calls the cryers kitty cats.

I sleep a little at a time because Mommy or Daddy has to make sure I take a bottle every two and a half hours. It usually hurts, and I spit a lot of it up. I'm starting to have a little awake time more often. Mommy or Daddy lays me on a pad during that time, and sometimes I move my arms and legs.

Today, Mommy says we're going to the doctor. I hope they won't hurt me. On the way there, as I begin dozing, my angel enters my sleep. I am very happy to have him near. He tells me, "You must be strong. The doctors at Cook's outpatient clinic have many necessary but painful tests for you over the next nine months. They aren't bad people; they don't want to hurt you. They must do the tests to help you." He calls them "neurologists" and "genetic specialists." I only understand "painful" and "doctors." I want to ask him what "people" means, but he keeps talking. "Over several visits and many months they will perform MRI tests that they will put you to sleep for." That one sounds easy. "There will also be blood tests, spinal taps, and muscle biopsies that they will have to put you to sleep for but will hurt afterward." Again I understand nothing, but those words make my body shudder. My angel, seeing my reaction, blankets and cloaks me in a warm and comforting light. He promises that this will give me strength.

When I awake, his cloak stays with me. My angel reassures me he will cloak me again on future visits. I feel a new, agonizing pain in my heart, though, when the doctors explain the procedures to my Mommy and she cries.

More trouble. My weight gain isn't keeping up with my growth "percentile." Mommy and Daddy have tried everything, short of the tummy button, to increase my nutrition and to spare me the pain of that surgery. I have even felt Mommy feeding me with an eye dropper repeatedly through the night in an attempt to replicate the tummy button's drip system. I pray my Mommy and Daddy choose to try the button. My angel will cloak me during the procedure.

In March Mommy and Daddy make an appointment with Cook Children's Hospital to insert my tummy feed button. The drip feeding should help Mommy and Daddy and me sleep through the night. The doctors put me to sleep for the procedure so I don't feel any pain, but I'm sure it is my angel's cloak that helps me. My mommy spends the night in the hospital with me, along with my angel.

The doctors put the feeding button above my own belly button and just below my ribs. It sticks up out of my skin, so I won't be able to lie on my tummy. At first it hurt when they attached the pump feed tube or the manual injection tube, though that part is getting better. But I still spit up a lot when I wake up in the morning. I hope that won't hurt my "percentile."

When I am six months old, Mommy and Daddy take me to another children's hospital, this one in Boston, Massachusetts. They say we are flying there, but it feels like riding in Mommy's car. I have seen my angel fly, and this kind of flying isn't like that either.

On the ride to the hospital as I fall asleep, my angel again appears. I tell him how relieved and grateful I am that he is here, and I nervously ask, "What are they going to do to me here?" He immediately cloaks me and tells me, "You will be visiting a pediatric neurologist for an MRI exam and blood tests. You will also be examined by an eye specialist to try to figure out why your eyes don't work right." Other than my angel I see only a dark fog. I ask my angel, "Why can I see you when I can't see anyone else?" Instead of answering my question, he asks me, "What do you see when you look at me?" I reply, "A light, a glow, that is pure and radiant and has ever-changing intensity and dimension moving freely around and over me without sound until you speak. When you cloak me, I don't feel you; I feel only warmth and security."

Then I ask what he sees when he looks at me. He answers, "I see a being, an infant human, a very small person made of flesh and blood embodying a soul." The only word I understand is "small." I ask what the word "person" means. He replies that I, also my mommy, daddy, brother, sisters and other similar language-voices are persons, are people. At that moment it becomes clear that all voices are persons, like me. The voices aren't spirits like my angel; they are people like me! Mommy is like me. I just can't see her. Mommy is like me!

Our trip to Boston is painful but quick. Both doctors will continue trying to figure out why my brain isn't communicating with either my eyes or my body to give me control over sight and movement. The tests give them no quick answers. I sleep on the plane all the way home.

My family calls this time of the year "summer." It's so hot I cannot tolerate being out during the day, so Mommy takes me outside in the early evenings and swings with me on the glider in the front yard. There she visits with other people and watches over brother and sisters and other children playing with them out front. Sometimes brother and sisters come up to me and talk or shove things in front of my face and tell me about what they are. I don't understand much of what they say, but I like hearing their loud voices. Now, I enjoy brother Tyler putting his face close to mine and saying "Booo!" loudly. It even makes me chuckle. That's how my summer goes each day. I am joyful not to have doctors' tests for this summer time.

When I go in for my weight check-ups, the doctors aren't happy with my "percentile." The overnight drip feedings seem to fill my tummy too much, so it hurts and I spit up a lot. My mommy worries a lot about my tummy's intolerance to food. The doctor encourages her to increase my feedings to give me more nutrition and help me gain weight, but she's torn about doing that since it will cause me more pain and make me spit up more. I wish my tummy liked my nutrition.

Some exciting family news arrives. Aunt Katie has given birth to a baby boy they named Brady. Everyone says he's a miniature of his daddy, Uncle Brandon. His big sister Briley can't understand why he sleeps so much—she doesn't know a lot about babies yet. The whole family gathered at the hospital to witness and welcome him, like they did for me! It is another blessed event for our family.

The doctors at Cook Children's are recommending that my current feeding button be replaced with a dual-function feeding button. It's called a "J" button. It has two feed ports: one directs food to my tummy like my present button, and the other sends it right to my small intestine. They think this system will increase my nutrition intake and reduce my spitting up. Mommy and Daddy agree, and after the procedure is complete, Mommy and I spend the night at Cook's.

Soon it is time for my nine-month tests at Cook's outpatient clinic. These will be very painful. My angel appears to me and explains that the doctors will compare the first three months of tests to the tests done today. Then all these tests will be combined and compared to my upcoming twelve-month tests. The final combined results will be used to map my progress and determine my root biological dysfunction and prognosis. The only words I understand are "tests" and "doctors."

I complain to my angel, "You didn't answer my question, when we were in Boston. Why can I see you when I can't see others?"

"The reason," he begins, "is that I am no longer a being of earth but rather one of heaven. Angels emit the purest form of light, unlike any energy on earth. Even those without sight can see us and those without hearing can hear us. This, of course, is if we wish them to. Oh, I hear the nurse coming to get you for the tests. I must cloak you...."

"But wait," I shout, "you said you're no longer a being of earth." "Shhh," he interrupts, "I must cloak you now."

I sleep all the way home after the visit. I'm so grateful for my angel. His cloaking dulls the most excruciating pain enough for me to tolerate it. He also comforts me by filling my mind with rapid sounds and visions of beings and surroundings from both the earthly and heavenly realms that lie beyond my darkened eyes. These temporary distractions help me overcome even my daily pain. I wonder if any of the earthly beings in these visions are my family members or other voices around me.

Now that we are back home, we witness the summer's end. We swing on the front-yard glider, listening to the voices and laughter of the children, ours and others from around the block. Summer's heat is long in retreat, and the fall air is cool and smells sweet. My brother and sisters are talking about getting pumpkins. We already have that woof woof and the crying kitties. Do we have room for pumpkins, too?

3

MAKING A DIFFERENCE FOR OTHERS

It happens suddenly, sharp and very painful. "MY LEG! MY LEG! Angel! Angel! Help me," I cry out. He appears and quickly cloaks me from the worst agony of this sudden pain. Mommy was only moving me at the time.

"TRENT, WHAT'S WRONG! I'm here, Trent. I'm here," Her voice is filled with alarm, concern, and confusion. I am crying loudly and screaming. Mommy slides her arm under me to pick me up, which rekindles my pain again. Mommy can't see what's wrong. I think, "If only I could say, 'My leg! My leg!,' she would know what to do to help me."

When we arrive at Cook Children's Hospital emergency room, the doctors examine me and determine the pain is in my left leg. They order x-rays, which show a double fracture of the bone. When they question Mommy about what happened, she replies, "I have no idea. Trent was asleep and quiet. When I started moving him and picking him up for his feeding, he suddenly began screaming."

The doctors put a partial cast on my leg and tell Mommy that they are required to report infant fractures to Child Protective Services. They explain that CPS will interview her and that I will have to spend the night at Cook's for observation. I can tell how terrible Mommy feels because I hear her crying. She stays overnight with me, but the emergency doctors and CPS-voices frightened her. It is agonizing for her to think she might have hurt me or that they might take me away from her. She did nothing wrong; she loves me.

The CPS-voice counsels with my primary doctors and reviews my records and x-rays. They determine that I have brittle-bone disorder as a result of inadequate nutrition intake. I just can't eat enough and keep it all down. My parents are devastated by this new development.

Not only is it a major setback in my progress, but it worries them on a practical level. How will they lift, hold, or embrace me without accidentally hurting me? Eventually CPS closes their file, and we can get back to our home routine. As for me, I get a cool cast out of it, full of stickers and writing that everyone puts on it to help me get well quicker.

Now my family and all my aunts, uncles, and cousins are talking about some kind of muddy run. They say Mommy and Daddy, brother, sisters, and all my cousins are going to run a race through mud pits and obstacles. This run's goal is to raise money for a charity. All my extended family and supporters call themselves "Trent's Team." That's me! We all have shirts that say that, too.

This week some strange things have started happening around here. My angel tells me it is called Halloween. Tonight my brother, sisters, and all kinds of other children and some parents will dress up in scary or funny costumes. Then they go to neighbors' homes and ring their doorbells. When the neighbors answer their door, the kids yell out, "Trick or treat!" That means if you don't give us a treat, we'll play a trick on you. Most of the time the neighbors hand out treats like candy or snacks. I don't understand any of it.

Early today the members of "my team"—my brother, sisters, and cousins—meet at Uncle Eric and Aunt Cathy's home to call our extended family and friends around the country requesting donations for Kidd's Kids, the mud-run charity. My team, in turn, will run an obstacle course through the mud to earn the money everyone pledged. The response is unbelievable; all the contributors are extremely generous. Not only is my team very excited, but our parents are very, very humbled by this outpouring of love and care.

My Aunts Cathy and Bec tell the team that the money raised is going to a charity started by Kidd Kraddick, a local radio personality. Kidd's Kids sends terminally ill children and their families to Give Kids The World, a wonderful retreat in Orlando, Florida, that provides families with a free week-long escape to fun and games at their facility. In addition, they give the families free passes to all the area theme parks, including Disney World, Universal Studios, Sea World, Busch Gardens, and others.

It is November 2010, and the day of the mud run is finally here. Mommy wakes me early so she can feed me before we leave. She says Daddy is packing the car with coolers, snacks, towels, chairs, my shade canopy, and my stroller. Tyler, Triny, and Tori are excited and louder than usual.

As we drive to the event, I hear Daddy ask the kids, "What do you think the mud run is going to be like?" Tyler describes it as large swampy ponds and ditches with booby traps and snakes. Triny thinks the course will have shallow ponds and a creek with turtles she can catch to take home. Tori paints the course as a garden with a path that she will follow while picking flowers for Mommy.

When we arrive at the event in north Fort Worth, we gather with aunts, uncles, cousins, grandparents, and family friends on top of a levee overlooking the Trinity River. The mud-run course stretches out along the bottom lands adjacent to the river. Mommy and Daddy leave for the adult race, a 10K course. Other adults set up chairs and my shade canopy on the levee crown.

My angel is with me, describing the scene. Several of the adults are going down to the adult course to watch for Mommy and Daddy and cheer them on. There are hundreds of runners entered in the race with identifying numbers on their shirts. Starting times are staggered throughout the day, so runners leave the starting line in groups of about twenty.

The kids and cousins go down to the kids' course to check it out, but they follow Mommy and Daddy back to the top of the levee after the 10K. All the children are laughing loudly at Mommy and Daddy, who returned tired and thirsty, soaking wet, and covered in mud! The adults applaud them. Now it is time for the kids race to begin.

My angel continues to explain the events. About eighty kids gather at the starting line with their parents there to cheer them on. An air horn blasts and sets them off running to the first obstacle, a large, long, low, muddy crawl pit. It has a low-hanging rope net over it, which forces the kids onto their bellies to wallow and wiggle through the pit. Uncle Eric runs along with Lindsey to help her through the obstacles. Aunt Katie goes with Tori, Matthew, and Briley. The older kids—Drew, Tyler, Darrion, and Kadden—arrive at the low-crawl pit in the first wave and slither right through it. Ashleigh and Trinity follow a short time later. Uncle Eric coaxes Lindsey through, and Aunt Katie's crew skirts the whole pit!

The second obstacle has several drainage pipes, twenty feet long by two feet in diameter, that the kids all have to crawl through. At the third obstacle there are elevated balancing beams they have to cross. Fourth come several long, deep, mud-filled trenches they must walk or swim through. (No snakes or booby traps yet though.) Running onto a large, high dirt pile, they climb over the top to a platform built into its side from which they launch themselves into a large and deep mud pit. Uncle Eric loses his balance while helping Lindsey into the pit and falls in on top of her, dunking them both. Aunt Katie's crew skirts the obstacle again!

The last obstacle is another large pile of dirt with a mud slide on one side giving them a ride into another mud pit. Then they reverse the course, repeating each obstacle back to the finish line. By the end they are thoroughly covered in multiple layers of mud.

When they are finished, Trent's Team rinses off some of the layers of mud by splashing and rolling in a large rain puddle. They laugh at how much mud everyone has accumulated on their bodies and exchange stories about the run. Once they are a little cleaner, they run up the levee to gather near me for pictures. Afterward, everyone continues to regale their parents with stories while they have drinks and snacks. With the races ended, people pack up and head off to the parking lot for free showers.

This shower isn't anything like at home. Because it has to accommodate hundreds of mud-covered runners, the fire department provides a large tanker engine with a water cannon mounted on top. A dozen or more adults and kids line up at a time and, facing the cannon shower, slowly turn in their tracks to wash the mud off their clothes, hair, and skin. Did I mention the water was cold? It was the perfect ending.

The contributions for Kidd's Kids earned by Trent's Team totaled $3,500. God Bless All!

My angel tells me Mommy and Daddy are receiving some long-awaited good news. Months ago, when I was first admitted to Cook Children's Hospital for testing, a social service agent helped them apply for Medicaid. They needed assistance to pay the huge medical bills for the ongoing testing to find out what's wrong with me. But before assistance could be approved, the agent told them, the doctors would need to determine a substantiated medical diagnosis. Unfortunately, the long process of medical testing to get a diagnosis would have to be paid for by Mommy and Daddy and their insurance. For that reason Mommy, Daddy, and I have traveled over the past nine months to various hospitals and clinics and endured a great number of tests in order to get that diagnosis.

Even though no diagnosis of my condition has yet been made, our family does meet the testing criteria established by Medicaid. So the agent is notifying Mommy and Daddy that since no diagnosis or prognosis can be determined, Medicaid will cover all further testing and treatments. They will also provide any equipment required, like my wheel chair. Finally, they will pay for respite care. The news is a great relief to my mommy and daddy.

In late November they remove my cast, and my leg feels good again. Now it's time for my twelve-month visit to Cook's outpatient clinic. My angel again helps me through the painful tests that will be compared to previous tests. The doctors will contact Mommy and Daddy when the final report is ready and will set up a meeting to review the results. I can tell Mommy and Daddy are worried about what the report will say.

In the meantime Mommy and Daddy have a surprise for our family. In celebration of my first birthday, we're going to spend the weekend in a cabin at a place called Broken Bow Lake. I'm just glad to be going anywhere with my family that isn't a hospital or a clinic.

I sleep most of the way there; Mommy wakes me only once to feed me. When we arrive at the cabin, she carries in my seat and sets me on the floor of the screened-in porch. My parents unload the car while Tyler, Triny, and Tori excitedly run all over. I notice the air smells different: it has a sweetness to it. The birds have louder voices, too. That night my family sings "Happy Birthday" to me and then the "Sto lat, sto lat" song. It has funny jumbled words that don't make any sense to me. My angel explains it's a traditional Polish birthday song wishing the person will live to be a hundred years old. Later that evening the kids play in what Mommy calls a "hot tub" on the back porch. Much later, when the kids and I are supposed to be sleeping, I hear Mommy and Daddy playing and laughing in the hot tub. I revel in their joy.

The next day we all go hiking, which seems a lot like walking to me. Mommy carries me in a pack that straps to her front. Tyler, like every other time he's outside, finds a long stick and plays what he calls "Ninja warrior" throughout the hike. Triny and Tori collect jewels (stones), roly-polies, leaves, shells, and of course flowers. To say the least, it is a noisy hike. But that's my family. I enjoy our time at the cabin very much.

When we get back, Mommy and Daddy meet with the doctors from Cook's outpatient clinic for my review and prognosis. The doctors tell them, "Trent has an unknown neurological disorder and possible metabolic dysfunction. We're sorry we can't provide better answers." The words "unknown" and "possible" crush my parents. How will the doctors ever find a treatment for my condition if they can't identify the cause? At this point, they can only recommend further testing with a metabolic genetic clinic in Houston. My parents are saddened by the lack of answers and the need for me to endure further testing.

When we return home, they somehow put on happy faces and voices and declare to us kids, "Today, we will start to prepare for celebrating Christmas! All else will keep until next year." That declaration immediately catches my angel's attention. He zips all around me and excitedly confides, "I must tell you *all* about Christmas." I have never seen him excited before. He has always appeared calm, strong, and protective. This Christmas must really be something.

When he finally settles down, he begins telling me the story of the birth of our savior, the Christ Child, the Son of God. Then he explains to me what this event means to all of humankind from that moment forward. My angel also reveals a few memories of his life as a being of earth: the excitement and joy of Christmas, the holy reverence of the occasion, and the joy of exchanging gifts in imitation of the three kings bringing gifts to the Christ Child. "Our home was full of Christmas decorations, music, delicious smells, laughter, and love," reminisces my angel. I am thoroughly enjoying Christmas already.

I ask my angel if he will tell me more of his life as a being on earth. He replies, "This season focuses on celebrating the birth of Jesus. I will tell you more about myself in the new year."

My family spends Christmas Eve at each of my grandparents' homes, along with all my aunts, uncles, and cousins. We first go to Bapcia and Dzia Dzia's home, where my kids and all the cousins love to play in their back yard. When they all eventually come in, they bring with them loads of noise and excitement.

Just before dinner, we partake in the Polish tradition of sharing "oplatki," the breaking of bread in the form of a wafer. Everyone in the family, including children, is given a wafer to share. Family members then mix and greet other members: they exchange a piece of wafer, praise and bless each other, then consume the wafer. They continue until everyone has been blessed by everyone else. My angel listens attentively to the many blessings and conversations.

After Bapcia announces it's time for dinner, Uncle Eric leads the family in a prayer of gratitude for the bounty God has shown us. He ends by wishing Jesus a happy birthday. The sumptuous meal the families share is topped only by the wondrous opening and exchanging of gifts. My angel explains that the shouts and screams of joy are quite normal and goes on to describe what gift has created the current outburst. It is very confusing to me, until Mommy says, "This gift's for you, Trent." She places something with a soft, furry covering against my face, and it tickles. Then she presses one of the paws, and the soft, furry thing says, "Hi, Trent! My name is Scout, and I love you." When he talks or plays music,

I can see a very faint glow of light blink. I know he will give me a great deal of comfort in painful times ahead.

At MiMi and Pop Pop's we enjoy more family traditions of this wonderful Christmas experience, but on the way home my angel tells me, "I have to leave you, but only temporarily. I am going to observe my earth family's Christmas celebrations. If you need me, though, I will be only a breath away." I tell him, "I am so happy you are going to see your family at this special time. I will be all right. Scout is with me."

Christmas morning comes, and I wake to cries and yells of joy as the kids open their gifts from under the tree. Mommy says they are from "Santa." I'll have to ask my angel about Santa when he returns.

We all attend church later that morning. It is a holy and solemn gathering of the faithful. We witness the word and participate in song. Happy Birthday, Jesus!

4

FINDING MY LAUGHTER

My angel returns around midday on Christmas. His glow is more radiant. He says, "Watching and observing my earth family now and then has that effect on me." I ask, "Do you want to leave and be around them always?" My angel laughs and says, "No. *You* are my priority." When I ask what "priority" means, he answers, "My sole responsibility. I am only YOUR angel." I feel tears on my cheek. I have cried while in pain or when frightened before, but this is the first time I cry for joy.

I ask him, "Can your family see you now?" He replies, "No. They see me only in pictures, memories, and dreams. But one day we will all be together again." Curious, I wonder, "Why did you leave them and become a heavenly being?"

He answers, "Not by choice. I was very sick with a terrible disease called cancer most of my five years as an earth being. God ended my suffering and brought me home, to His home. When I arrived I was greeted by family members who had passed on long before me. In God's home, I was healthy and whole again.

"After a short time God summoned me. I was awestruck in His presence. He said He had an important assignment for me. I was to be granted angel status and assigned as the guardian to a special soul. He explained that this new soul, presently a fetus, would be born but sadly would not be whole. His name would be Trent, and I would be given the privilege of comforting and protecting him on his most painful journey through earthly life."

I exclaim to my angel, "God must really love me!"

As night falls upon our Christmas, it is time for me to be hooked up to my feeding pump for the night. Mommy kisses me and places Scout by my side. Although she can't see him, my special angel is nestled in on my other side.

A few days later, when I wake up, Mommy greets me, saying, "Happy New Year, Trent. I prayed this morning that the new year will bring us answers and bring you a pain-free, healthier, and happier life." I don't understand the words "New" and "Year," but her prayer sums up my hopes, too.

As January ends, news comes from my Aunt Cathy that she and Uncle Eric have welcomed a foster child by the name of Marhia into their home. Marhia is three days old and suffers from a cocaine addiction her drug-addicted mother transmitted to her while she was still in the womb.

My angel is at my side when the news comes, and he explains what the words mean. He tells me that Marhia must go through months of painful drug detoxification to rid her body of the drugs. The thought of a mommy doing this to her baby deeply disturbs me. I weep for Marhia. My angel says that it is God's will that Marhia survive her birth and the trauma surrounding it so He will use that experience to bring about good in her life. Through foster care, he continues, she will find a loving family to care for her, love her, and help her through physical and emotional difficulties.

My angel sadly states the awful truth: "Many mommies and daddies don't deserve to become parents. Some change with maturity and spiritual growth. But many only bring pain, suffering, and even death to their children." I cry out, "DEATH! You're saying they intentionally bring death upon their children?"

With a deep sadness reflected in his light, he answers, "Yes, Trent, people struggle each day with an internal battle between good and evil. Some parents make terrible decisions and allow evil to prevail in their actions and lives. Evil comes in many forms: some become irrationally angry; some are jealous or envious of others, some succumb to hatred. Such evil is fostered by money, drugs, selfishness, even mental illness. When pressured, human beings strike out at whatever they see as the cause of their pain. Sometimes that is a child, and the results can be deadly.

"However, most of the children who die each year, and I know this will be hard for you to hear, die at the hands of their own mommies who choose to end their pregnancies. It's called abortion, Trent, and it's an all-too-common practice, I'm afraid."

When I ask, "How?," he answers, "By various means. In the very beginning, they use a morning-after pill. Later, when the fctus is growing in the womb, they use drugs. Later yet, the baby is pulled apart inside the womb and vacuumed out by a doctor. The most horrific, sinful act—called 'late-term abortion'—is when the child is traveling through the birth canal, and the doctor kills him as he is being born."

In great sorrow, I ask, "Why does this happen?" My angel sighs and says, "For many, deeply selfish, and callous reasons. They say they're too young to raise a child, it's inconvenient at this time, they have no husband or partner to help raise the child, they can't afford the child, the child is the wrong sex, or the child has a medical condition or deformity. The present laws allow these vile acts."

"Why does God not stop it?" I question. He responds, "God has revealed His laws and the rules of charity by which humanity should live, codified in the Ten Commandments and exemplified in the Holy Bible. But God also loves human beings so much that He will not force them to do anything. Instead, He gives them free will so that they may choose whether or not they will follow charity and wisdom and be with Him. If humankind abides by God's laws, they will attain the glory of His kingdom. If they abandon God's law, as in abortion, and do not repent, they choose death and destruction."

"Do these aborted children of God have angels?" I want to know. "Yes," he replies. "These aborted children represent the holiest of the holy in their short time on earth. They gave their all to God and spiritually walked with His Son Jesus. So God asks them to be the guardians of other babies in the womb who are in danger; He sends them to protect the sanctity of life while on earth." He also let me know that Marhia will be safe and happy because she is in a loving home with people who will take good care of her.

My Aunt Cathy told Mommy that my cousins Drew, Ashleigh, Lindsey, and Matthew are excited that Marhia is coming into their home. I am curious, so I ask, "Do all people have guardian angels?" "All people who retain their souls have guardian angels" was his reply. "Those who choose to be led through life by satanic demons of envy, hatred, anger, lust, gluttony, sloth, or pride forfeit their souls." I tell my angel, "I hope I never encounter a soulless person." He says, laughing, "It's my job to make sure you don't."

One day I hear Triny say, "Mommy, will you cut out my heart? I want to put it on this card." Because of what my angel has said, I momentarily panic, thinking she may have fallen into evil ways. My angel quickly assures me the heart is a paper one Triny has drawn for a valentine card she made for Mommy. He goes on to explain the meaning of St. Valentine's Day. I wish I could give Mommy a valentine.

When March arrives, it is time to travel to Houston and visit the metabolic genetic doctor. We go in the car; my angel explains that I am going to have a physical examination and a blood test. He says the doctor will send off samples for analysis, and in about two months, a report will return detailing my genetic code and the arrangement of chemical constituents in molecules of my DNA. My mind is reeling. My angel can tell I am lost and confused. "In short," he says, "the test checks to see if there is an 'error' deep inside you that makes you unable to control your body movements and your sight and makes your tummy hurt. If there is an error, it can be found and fixed."

My angel cloaks me. It doesn't seem that the difficulties of the day warrant cloaking. Perhaps he senses another imminent threat. When the tests are complete, the doctor tells Mommy and Daddy they will need to return when the report is ready for review. All of this is so very hard on my parents. I wish my angel could cloak them from pain.

As Mommy picks me up to put me in my car seat for the return home, I emit a piercing scream reminiscent of the pain at my first leg fracture. She cries out to Daddy, "No, no, it can't be! Shane, I'm afraid Trent has another fracture in his leg."

The pain isn't as bad this time, thanks to my angel's foresight. Once we return home, the doctors at Cook Children's order x-rays that reveal another fracture higher up on my left leg. I get another cast. No CPS notification is required this time because Cook's has a record of my brittle-bone history. In fact, they have provided my parents with a written assessment of my bone condition to give to any emergency personnel caring for me at any medical facility.

One day of no particular importance, as my angel is reminiscing about events within his short life on earth, he starts singing. When I ask what the song means, he says it's just a silly song his grandmother taught him. He says, "I'll use your name and show you. It goes like this:

Trent Trent bo bent

bo nana fana fo fent

me my mo ment, Trent!"

As he goes on with the song, I start to feel an uncontrollable laugh, a very loud, exuberant, deep belly laugh, roaring up within me. I have never laughed like that before. When my angel finishes, I finally stop laughing. I ask him what it means. He says, "Nothing. It's just for fun. You can insert any name in the song and change the rhyme." I begin to laugh uncontrollably again as I think to myself what a perfect song for me: no meaning, just fun!

While I am laughing so loud and uncontrollably, Mommy and Aunt Bec, who are close by, are drawn to me in amazement and began laughing with me. They don't know what initiated my laughter. They just rejoice in my exuberance, laugh with me, and share the news of my laughter with many, near and far away.

5

MORE REASONS TO SMILE

In June of 2011, Mommy receives a call from the Houston doctor, who says that the first results are negative, or indeterminate. She asks that we return for retesting and further analysis of new blood samples. Mommy agrees to the request. At the same time, my doctor here isn't happy with my insufficient weight gain. My "J" button isn't helping my nutrition intake or reducing my spitting up. My tummy still hurts a lot, too.

As providence would have it, my tummy button somehow pops out. Sometimes I flail my arms and legs uncontrollably. I must have caught my button with my arms and pulled it out. When Mommy and Daddy take me to Cook Children's emergency to have it reinstalled, the doctor gives them the option of returning to the original single-port button. Since the "J" wasn't helpful, they choose the original. I am allowed to go home that night.

The Houston visit is not very painful. After the doctor reviews my negative blood test report with my parents, she explains that the blood samples drawn today will again be forwarded to a laboratory to analyze additional molecule groupings or something like that. I don't understand what she means. In two months we will know the results.

At home, we begin to repeat our summer routine. The days are hot, so I stay inside until the sun is low in the sky and the front-yard glider is shaded. The doctors have been changing my medications to try to reduce my pain or mask it, but my tummy still hurts. What cheers me up and makes me laugh uncontrollably is the happy, silly song my angel sings to help me.

In midsummer my whole family takes a trip to Illinois to visit the extended families of both my mommy's parents. It is a pleasant break from the heat in Texas. I get to spend most days outside in the cooler weather. In the evenings my kids and my cousins chase and catch fireflies and put them in jars. My angel explains that these little flying bugs periodically glow like fire as they slowly rise from the grass. He jokes that they resemble a miniature angel convention as they light up throughout the yard. My angel flashes a momentary image of the scene in my mind for me to see and enjoy. I smile because it is so beautiful.

While we're here, we stay with my mommy's cousin Kristin, her husband Fred, and daughters Abby and

Natalie. We also celebrate my Great Bapcia's eighty-third birthday, where everyone sings the "Sto lat, sto lat" song. It's wonderful to visit with my big extended family—they are all full of love and care! On the way home to Texas, Mommy notices my sniffling and says I must have caught a cold in Illinois. But as far as I'm concerned, you have to take a little bad with all the good.

In late August the Houston doctor calls Mommy and sadly reports that the second round of test results are also negative. She apologizes for not being able to determine the root cause of my condition. This is another disappointing dead-end for my parents.

In early fall Mommy receives a phone call from a representative of the TV show "Curb Appeal" on HGTV (Home and Garden Television Productions), who tells her that her name was submitted for a possible TV episode. They ask Mommy to submit a video of the front of our home in which she explains what improvements she and Daddy think are needed and would like to see. If they choose her presentation, the show will remodel the entrance to our home and the front yard.

Mommy immediately agrees to forward the video. This opportunity happens because a friend of hers won a Grand Make-Over prize offered by HGTV and was asked to submit names of others who might benefit from the consolation prizes they are offering. God bless her for handing in Mommy's name.

Our whole family is excited, and we all appear in the video that pinpoints our difficulties. Mommy and Daddy have always been concerned about how they would manage getting me back and forth to the car or front yard when I'm eventually in a wheel chair. The uneven walkway and porch step pose real problems. If we win, the TV show would work to resolve them. My family prays hard that we'll be chosen.

Within three weeks of sending in the video, Mommy receives the call we've been praying for. The representative notes, "Trent's need for access to the house was the deciding factor in choosing your family for the make-over. We'll start the project in early January." We all feel extremely blessed.

My next doctor's appointment isn't until January, after my second birthday, at Cook's outpatient clinic. At least I have four months until the appointment. I don't want to think about it, because they do so many tests that are the most painful for me and my parents.

Throughout the remainder of the late Texas summer and into the cool of fall, my angel does his magic to keep me distracted from thinking about Cook's. I keep having lots of tummy pain, along with some new pain to endure. But he continues to sing his silly song, each time making me laugh loud and long. "The new pain you're experiencing," my angel tells me, "is a tooth slowly poking its way through the skin in your mouth. It's perfectly normal and will happen many times over in the next few years." This pain doesn't seem to worry

Mommy, so that's good. As I think about it, though, this tooth thing is the only normal development I've undergone in my life, and even it hurts. Go figure.

Halloween night has come and gone again, as have those pumpkins. That means it's time for the second annual mud run, and the excitement bubbles up in everyone in the family. The day is full of fun, laughter, and mud. My team members carry their banner proudly and revel in as much mud as they can. After all, this is the only time kids can get their clothes incredibly dirty and not get in trouble with their mommies.

To top off the day, the generous donors provide a significant contribution to families of children with terminal illnesses. Kidd's Kids receives $4,000 from Trent's Team. God bless them, every one.

Our family celebrates my second birthday at home. Mommy says, "There are lots of bugs in the air, so we are going to stay in today." I am a little confused; no one stayed in when there were fireflies everywhere. So my angel tries to explain, "Your mommy doesn't mean real bugs; she means there are viruses everywhere." I remain confused.

Our family once again begins preparing for the miracle of Christmas. All the traditional decorations and symbols, music, sweet smells, love, and laughter will escort in the holiest of nights.

It is during this time of preparation that my angel speaks to me of his experiences as a being of earth late in his illness. "My parents," he recounts, "met with the team of doctors that were managing my cancer treatment and battle. In the meeting, the doctors reviewed the history of my treatments and noted the lack of remission and the persistent advancement of my disease over the previous three years. It was clear the team had explored and implemented all known treatments and performed every surgical option that was available. Unfortunately, the cancer had advanced to stage four and my prognosis was terminal.

"Their summation was clinical, devoid of emotion and allowing no further discussion. It was a heartbreaking revelation for my parents. They knew the doctors had to conceal any emotion in order to give an accurate assessment. In doing so, the doctors were clearly handing over my final care to my parents and to God.

"Now my father and mother had to prepare themselves properly by means of their faith and with the reverent assistance of hospice services to accept the most difficult responsibility parents are sometimes called upon to shoulder. Day by day they had to comfort a fragile and dying child with unending love, compassion, and strength and escort him into the open arms of God."

Amazingly I understand every word he speaks. I also somehow understand why he is telling me his story at this time in my life. I cry for his parents' loss, and I pray for my parents, who are facing a most difficult, painful journey ahead.

Christmas is all I could hope for. The now-familiar traditions and blessings fill me with joy. I receive a gift of something called Yo Gaba Gaba. I'm not sure about it yet. The first time Daddy plays it for me, the music seems loud. I do faintly make out what I think are changing color tones that move to the music.

Mommy is worried, though, about my persistent congestion and now fever. The medication the doctor ordered isn't helping. So after New Year's she takes me to Cook Children's, where the emergency personnel check my condition and discover my congestion has progressed into pneumonia and RSV. After some consulting, the doctor in charge tells Mommy I need to be admitted for treatment and monitoring. We spend two nights in Cook's; on the third day the doctors tell my parents that the virus can't be treated with drugs. My immune system will have to fight it off on its own.

Worse yet, they tell Mommy and Daddy they are recommending I be enrolled in hospice care services. Those words momentarily rock their very souls. They fall to their knees in prayer; they seek guidance for the journey they face. I wish I could tell them not to worry for me. My angel has already prepared me for this day.

More Reasons To Smile

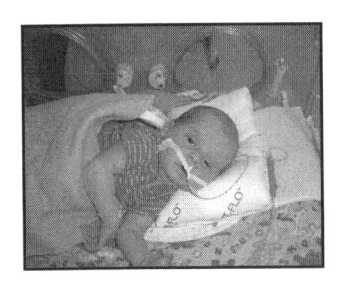

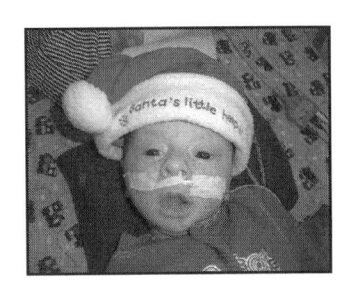

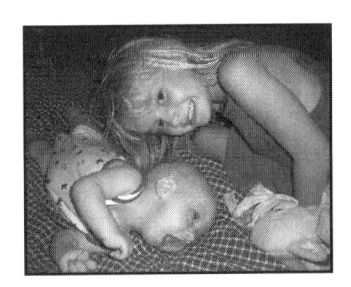

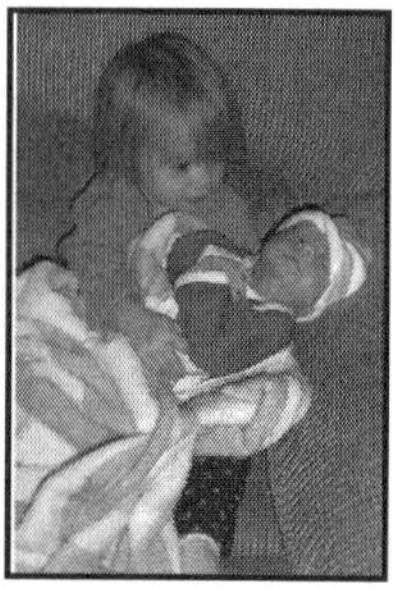

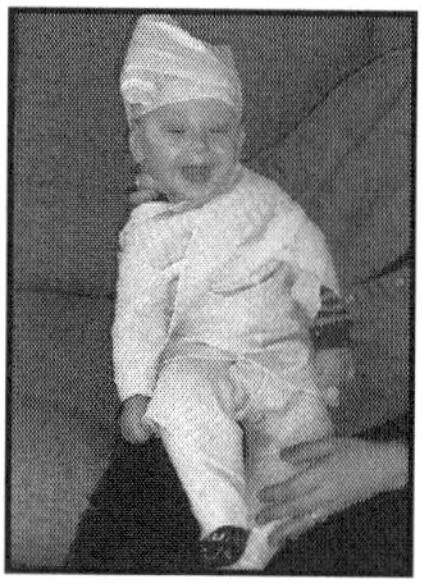

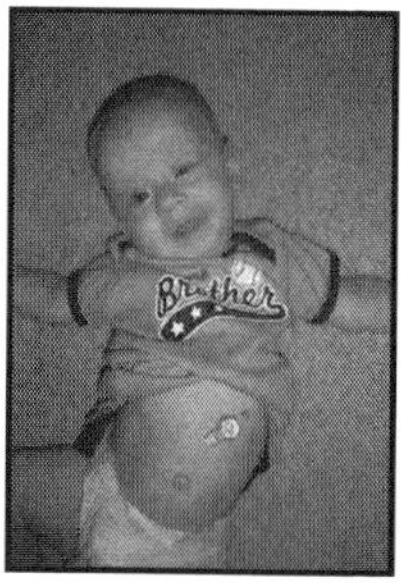
Brother

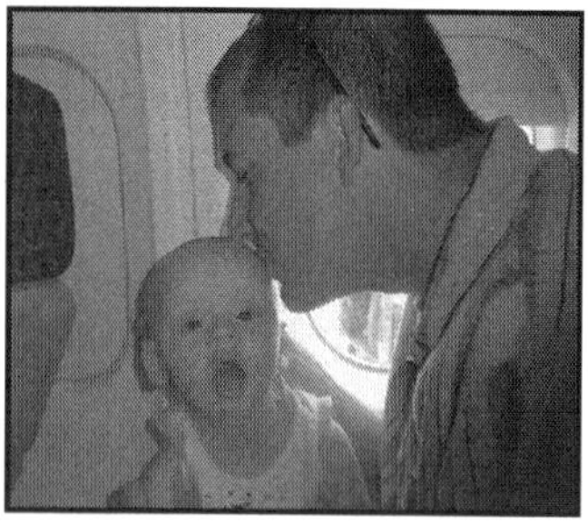

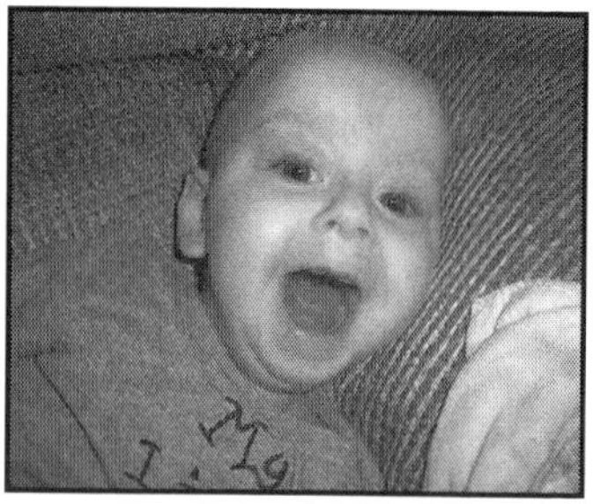

MORE REASONS TO SMILE 51

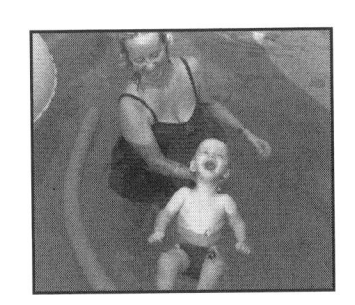

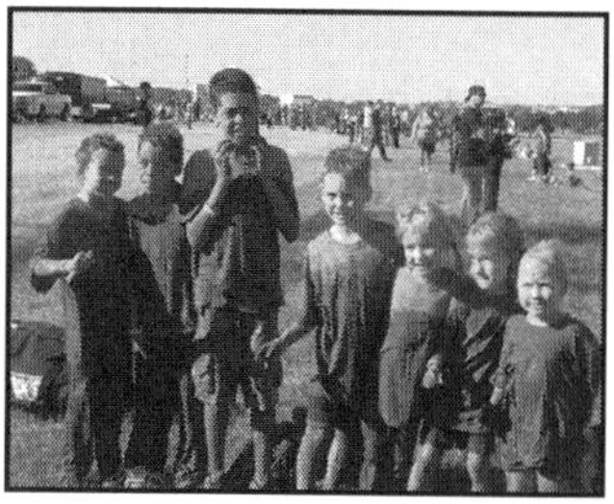

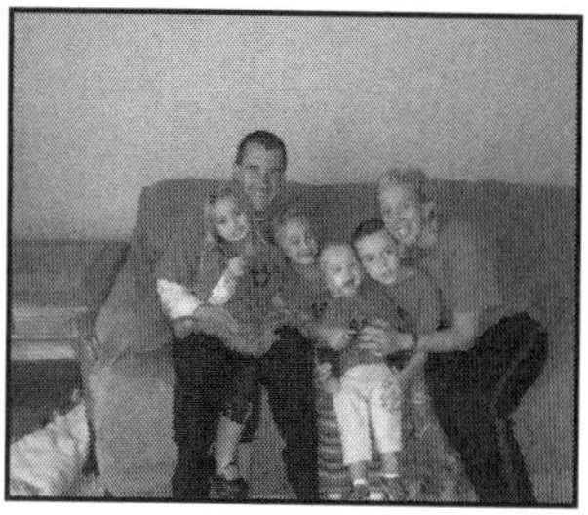

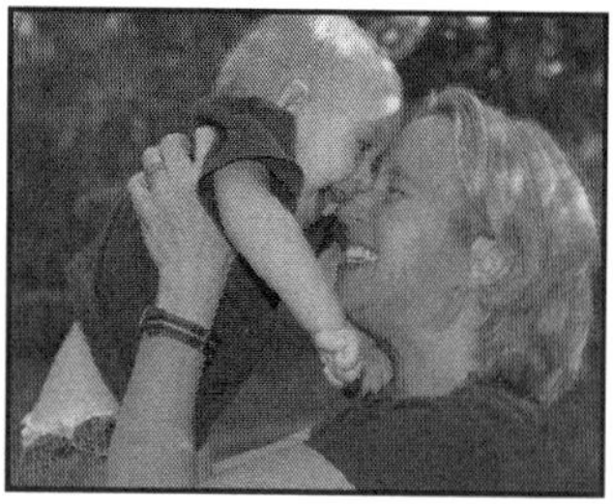

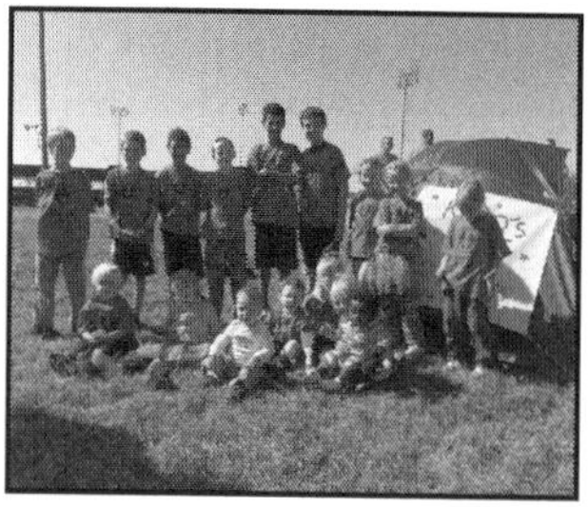

More Reasons To Smile 53

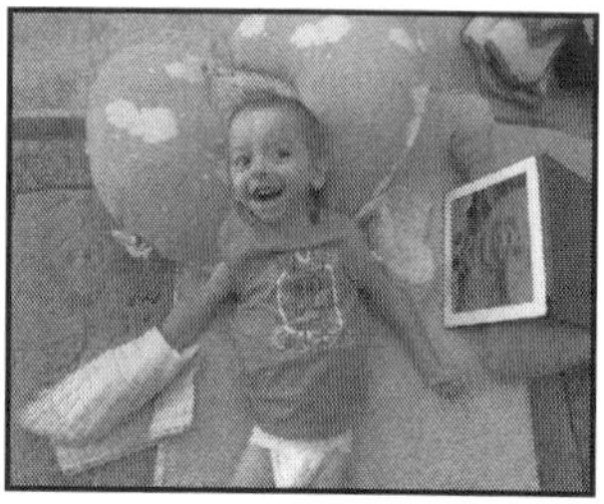

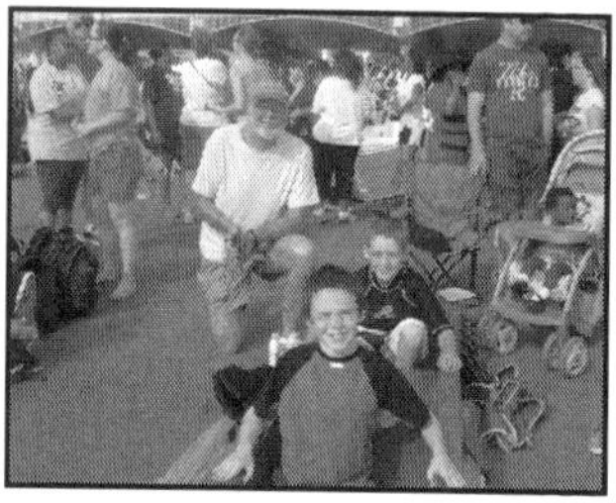

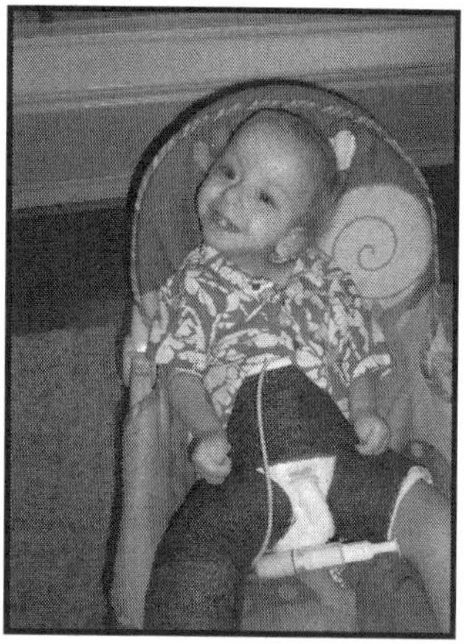

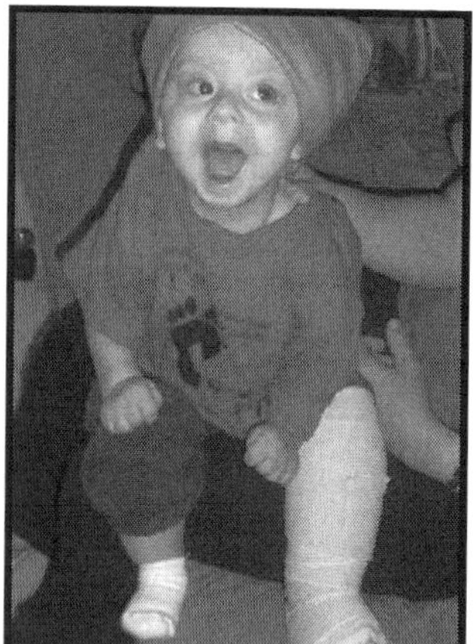

More Reasons To Smile

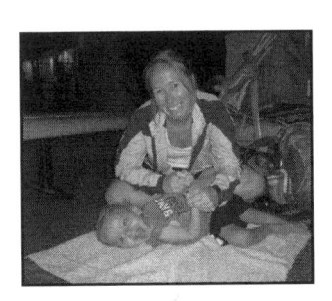

55

6

A BLESSING
FOR OUR FAMILY

As we drive home from Cook Children's, my angel comforts me. I ask, "What is the hospice service, and what will they do?" He begins by saying, "Hospice is a special organization of care providers that offer end-of-life assistance and care for earthly beings, for people. The organization is made up of paid professionals like doctors, nurses, therapists, counselors, and more. There are also volunteers who provide spiritual support and guidance such as priests, ministers, rabbis, and others. Other volunteers help in any capacity needed to fulfill their mission of easing suffering and aiding in the transition from this life to a heavenly one. The organization also provides the patient with medications, special-needs equipment, quality of life essentials, and more. All of them work with special angels at their side."

I can tell Mommy is overwhelmed; she has no previous involvement with hospice care and is uncertain how they can help. And she doesn't have my angel to explain and calm her fears. Once contacted, Hospice sends a gentle, empathetic, and nonintrusive army to provide care and assistance to me and my family. They are a blessing bestowed on us; we will be eternally grateful for their presence and assistance at this critical time.

Mommy calls Cook's outpatient clinic and cancels my final appointment for tests. I tell my angel how happy I am to hear that call. He replies, "There won't be any more testing. There will only be pain management as long as you need it."

A nurse stays with me twenty-four hours a day until my respiratory crisis subsides and I recover. God isn't finished with me here on earth! I remain on hospice care; the nurses are gone but will return whenever needed, and Hospice continues to provide medications, therapy, and moral support. My parents are so thankful and amazed by the generous assistance and loving care Hospice gives me and my family.

As I am recovering, the HGTV "Curb Appeal" representative, show host, and producer interview my parents. They want their input on what improvements to the front of the house will allow easier accessibility and benefit my movements now and in the future. Immediately, they discuss expanding the area along the driveway to accommodate the loading and unloading of a wheel chair. Next, they imagine a ramp to the porch so I can move effortlessly up to that level.

The show's host, while listening and taking notes, notices our old yet reliable glider. He asks Mommy if it is important to us, and she replies, "Yes. Trent and I sit on the swing each evening and watch the kids and their friends play out front." He continues writing notes and taking pictures. When he is finished, he says they will work up alternative design plans of the improvements they discussed for my parents to review in a few days. Later at home Daddy asks my kids what changes they would like out front. The general consensus is a tree house and a drinking fountain. My parents nix those suggestions.

Once the designs are complete, Mommy and Daddy meet the show host, producer, and the camera crew at a local restaurant where the crew films the presentation of the design plans to my parents. With the cameras rolling, my parents are taken through a before and after look at the front of their house.

The new improvements look remarkable, my angel tells me. New colonial-style lampposts placed on both sides of the driveway will give better night lighting. A flagstone walkway adjoining the driveway will provide a stable surface to load and unload a wheel chair. Then the walkway snakes along the front of our home gradually gaining height to blend evenly with an expanded front entry and spacious elevated patio area that reaches out into the front yard. Best of all, he says, the design depicts a beautiful colonial arbor with a big swing for me and Mommy in the middle of the patio. The downward sloping yard is terraced below the patio flagstone skirting with a matching retaining wall capped with flagstone at sitting height, though I'm not sure what all of that means. However, I know it will be wonderful that the wall forms a semicircular rock bench for my kids and others to sit and play on. My parents, both pleased and amazed at the functional yet very appealing improvements, are excited to get started. The producer lets them know demolition and construction will start in four weeks.

When February comes, it's time for the "Curb Appeal" project to begin. The film crew sets up in the cool, early morning, joined by some family members who have come to see them start. I stay inside recuperating throughout the project, but my angel eagerly reports everything that happens. I think there is still a lot of little boy in him.

First, a parade of trucks rounds the corner and drives up to our house. Neighbors come out to see what is going on. Suddenly there are materials, equipment, and workers everywhere. After a short speech by the TV host and some introductions, the work crews begin demolishing the old walkway and digging out the expanded area next to the drive. They're also trimming the trees and pulling out shrubbery. Brother Tyler is getting a true bird's-eye view by perching himself in a large mimosa tree on the side of the yard. They work so quickly, my angel reports, that by the end of the day the workmen have everything formed up and have delivered truckloads of topsoil and sand.

On day two, they begin the concrete work in preparation for something called flagstone overcapping. Over the next week, my angel reports that the crews have transformed the front of the house so it looks just like the initial project design. It is beautiful, he sighs, especially the arbor swing for Mommy and me.

While the construction is in full swing, I guess I am a little lonely and feeling down. My battle with pneumonia is probably to blame. Although my angel is not constantly with me, I know he is near. I know he would appear in a breath, as he always says, if I need him. It's just that I can't understand why he's so preoccupied with the project out front. The next time he returns to update me, I will ask him.

I don't have long to wait. It seems someone has cut a sprinkler line, whatever that is, and he comes to tell me about it. As he begins to recount the incident for me, I interrupt, asking him, "What is it that enthralls you about this project?" He answers, "I have good memories of my fourth year as a being of earth. Between the darker days of my disease, my father would take me along to his job site to see and learn about construction work. He was a contractor who did projects like yours and much bigger ones, too. Watching the work they're doing out in the front of the house takes me back to what my daddy taught me about his life's work."

I ask, "Why did your daddy do this work?" He laughs a little and says, "Because he loved what he did and it provided a good living for our family. You see, I also loved what my daddy did and wanted, when I was old enough, to learn all about his trade and work with him." I understand now that his intense interest in the work out front is, for him, a reconnection with his father.

When I ask him what *my* daddy does for work, he tells me, "Your daddy is a police officer." I ask him to explain more. So he describes my daddy's job: "Your daddy works to help people and protect them from any harm that others might wrongly wish to do to them. It's a very important and noble profession." I think, Wow! My daddy's noble! How cool! I would like to be like him.

With the work on the front of the house complete, my parents have a party, an open house with a delicious buffet to thank our HGTV "Curb Appeal" friends and the contractors. They also invite family, friends, and neighbors. Everyone there is amazed at the finished product. Daddy gives a speech thanking all those involved in bringing this beautiful gift to our family. The production crew has the cameras rolling for the party, and the film crew interviews various family members and guests to include on the TV episode when it airs.

It was, all in all, a fun and blessed experience. We will continue to enjoy our beautiful front yard and mine and Mommy's swing through those spring, summer, and fall evenings ahead. [The "Curb Appeal" episode about Trent's home can be found at www.hgtv.com/curb-appeal/show.]

I start feeling better; I even burst out laughing a couple of times when my angel sings his silly song to distract me from my ongoing tummy pain. I lost some weight while overcoming the pneumonia and am at twenty pounds, way below my "percentile." I'm well enough, though, to continue my therapy sessions. The therapists come to our house to treat me, focusing on my vision, which isn't working, and, more importantly, on the muscles around my joints. They exercise my limbs, hands, and fingers to keep them from stiffening and locking up. I seem to require a lot of maintenance.

My Yo Gaba Gaba video helps me a lot. The music and the changing light patterns that I can faintly see captivate me. I begin thrashing my arms and legs to the rhythm of the music. My kids say it's my version of break dancing. Sometimes while dancing, I somehow scoot away from my Yo Gaba Gaba player and then I fuss a lot until someone repositions me close to it again.

One day in March when I am lying on the sofa and flailing to Yo Gaba Gaba, I scoot myself right off the couch. I slip right between the bumper cushions laid out to stop me. The pain is a familiar one. When Mommy quickly answers my cries and picks me up, she realizes I may have another broken bone. The Cook Children's emergency room doctor takes x-rays and determines I have a fracture on my right leg this time, high up near my hip. He fits me with a lower-body cast that immobilizes my right leg by extending the cast over my upper left leg. My angel laments that this will really put a crimp in my break dancing.

In early spring our family grows when Aunt Cathy and Uncle Eric formally adopt Marhia, who seems to have overcome her induced addiction with few apparent side effects. To do so well, she has required a lot of love and prayers, an attentive and loving family, various therapies, and, of course, her own angel.

The family court judge, Geraldine Smith, goes out of her way to include in the proceedings our entire family, all of whom have come to witness this blessed event. Marhia, who has just turned one, is wearing a pretty yellow dress. As the judge begins, she asks Marhia's soon-to-be-daddy to hand Marhia over to sit in the judge's lap through the proceedings. She then invites Drew, Ashleigh, Lindsey, and Matthew to stand on either side of her. While the petition proceeds, Marhia is content to rock back and forth on the judge's lap and play with the gavel. At the end, the solemn oath to love, watch over, and care for Marhia repeated by her new parents is indeed sweet justice. You can tell Judge Smith loves her important work by the way she includes everyone in this important, joyful, family experience. We are so blessed!

7

SPRING HAPPENINGS

My angel thinks it is funny that my kids signed their names on my cast. He wishes he could, too. He keeps me informed about my kids' school lessons and their school-related activities. He tells me that Mommy has given them a project to collect or catch and identify various plant and critter specimens as part of their science curriculum. My kids are excited at the opportunity to hold school outside in the park instead of at home today.

He explains, "Your kids are part of a growing number of children being schooled at home. Homeschoolers are taught mainly by one or both parents, following a curriculum developed for each grade level by a homeschooling association." Some of my cousins are also homeschoolers. Mommy is my kids' teacher for the most part, but they and many other homeschoolers also attend "Classic Conversation" (CC) classes at our church community center in which various parents and volunteers teach the more critical aspects of math, science, language, and more.

Today, however, is a science field trip. We're all going with Mommy and Aunt Bec to the park to hike the trails collecting and catching our specimens. After arriving around mid-morning, we initially search for those specimens near the picnic area and east trail. At lunchtime my kids, loudly of course, share stories of the critters that got away and show each other the specimens they are keeping. After lunch we head down the west trail and, their favorite, the creek that runs along the trail, where they manage to catch a small turtle, some tadpoles in a cup, and a water bug. They also find some small shells and a rock that Tyler insists is an Indian arrowhead. The girls pick some flowers and leaves from the low branches of trees. Tyler chases some butterflies and catches some crickets and a green-shelled beetle.

With a successful afternoon hunt, it's now time to catalog their specimens. The critters that survived my kids' care are returned to the creek or the embankment along it. Aunt Bec gathers all the plant specimens to take home for the kids to look up, identify, and learn about. All the fresh cool air makes me sleepy and I nap at times. My angel inserts flash images of the day's events in my dreams, to my great pleasure. He calls it "dreaminating."

I develop a new medical condition in April that inexplicably deprives me of sleep. I constantly whimper and moan because of my distress. My nerves are frazzled to the point that I flinch and jerk uncontrollably. This condition goes on for a few days before my exhausted Mommy and Daddy notify Hospice, which immediately provides around-the-clock nursing care. They diagnose my condition as anxiety and begin treating it with medication. Although the first drugs don't help and a second medication makes it worse, my condition nonetheless improves enough after three more days that the hospice nurses can leave to help others.

My angel notices that Mommy and Daddy are rearranging the upstairs bedrooms. Triny and Tori share one bedroom and Tyler has another and the third room is left completely empty. We know it can't be for me. I have to be monitored during the night in case I gag or choke on my spit up, so I sleep in the downstairs den in a special bed that my Dzia Dzia made for me. The empty room remains a mystery.

My brother Tyler and cousin Drew are working with Dzia Dzia on designing and building a cardboard boat that the two boys will race in something called "The Cardboard Boat Regatta." My angel explains that the event, which takes place at the Hurricane Harbor water park in Arlington, will host well over a hundred entrants, including both youngsters and adults. Youth division participants are between the ages of eight and thirteen; participants fourteen and older compete in the adult division. For the youth division, boat entry categories include "Guppy" (crew of one to two), "Dolphins" (crew of three to five), and "Whale" (crew of six to ten). Tyler, who is eight, and Drew, who is ten, will race in the Guppy category.

When I ask what happens in a big boat race, my angel replies, "In each race, or heat, three boats are launched and entrants race through a horseshoe course in the wave pool. The winner of each heat advances until the last three contestants race against each other in the finals. Afterward, trophies are given to the first-, second-, and third-place winners in each category."

He reports that the boys have painted and named their two-person boat "Voyager." Before the race, they have practiced in a kayak in Drew's pool and in a lake at an area park. Tyler sits in the front, or bow, and is responsible for setting the paddling pace. In the rear, or stern, Drew is responsible for steering the boat through the course while paddling at the set pace.

The boat regatta race day has arrived, and my angel and I are both excited. Tyler and Drew spend the night at Dzia Dzia and Bapcia's house so they can arrive early at Hurricane Harbor together. They register their boat and number, then carry the cardboard vessel to their staging spot. My family—aunts, uncles, cousins, MiMi, Pop Pop, and some family friends—soon arrive. My angel promises to describe the scene and action for me as the morning unfolds.

Tyler, Drew, and some of the cousins wander through the sea of competitors' boats to check them out. There are 121 boats entered in all categories and age groups. Some of the boats are well engineered and highly detailed, my angel says, but most are built in a basic, box-shaped, flat-bottomed canoe style. While most look capable of handling the multiple heats, a few are questionable. Then there are a dozen or so that look either too fragile and risk sinking early or too top heavy and might flip over.

According to my angel, all the youth entrants use canoe or kayak paddles for propulsion. Some of the adults in the class 2 mechanical categories employ bicycle pedals and chain-driven paddle wheels or propellers for propulsion. All the various boats staged around the wave pool make for a very colorful sight, he says.

As the youth races are about to start, the announcer walks through the collection of boats, interviewing the crews and getting everyone excited. The starter group begins calling out boat numbers in groups of three, signaling the boat crews to move their boats to the starting area of the pool. The announcer calls out the boat names and numbers as they line up for each heat. The starter triggers an air horn blast that signals the start of each race and startles me. The fun commences!

The qualifying heats are exciting and full of laughter. The less capable craft slowly sink in mid-race or flounder and flip right after they are launched. Remarkably, my angel tells me, Tyler and Drew win their first three heats and qualify for the finals.

The final race includes two other crews: one of older boys and one of older girls. My angel delights in recounting the dramatic scene to me. At the horn blast, all three crews shove off and jump into their boats. Unfortunately, the girl in the stern slips while boarding and falls into the water. The bow member, who has no idea that her teammate fell out, starts paddling forward, while the one in the water frantically swims to try to catch the boat. In doing so, she crosses the path of Tyler and Drew's boat, causing them to stop and readjust their course. In the meantime the older boys paddle on unobstructed, taking the lead. Tyler and Drew try to catch up but fall short and come in second.

We all cheer them on and meet them at the finish line to congratulate them. Trophies are handed out, and high fives are plentiful at this fun event. We are all proud of their great performance in their very first boat regatta competition. "Voyager" has served the boys well. It survives the regatta, but, my angel sadly recounts, it will eventually meet its fate at the bottom of Drew's pool. Even as they accept congratulations, the boys already have new ideas for next year's boat.

Not long after the boat regatta, I again battle a respiratory infection. The hospice nurses help me through the worst part, staying with me day and night as they did before. As usual, my Aunt Bec helps Mommy and Daddy take care of me before and after hospice care.

Mid-spring is here, so the afternoons out front on the swing are still comfortable. The sounds and smells are different at this time of year. We sometimes have terrible storms bringing what Tori calls "thunderbooms" that shake the whole house and frighten me. When the weather clears up and Mommy takes me out into the night air, it smells fresher and sweeter.

Most mornings before dawn Mommy takes me with her when she goes running. She straps me into the jogging stroller, and off we go. Next to my swing time with Mommy this is my second favorite part of the day. Or is it night? The breeze is cool, and the neighborhood is asleep and quiet. It's quality time with Mommy.

My angel tells me, "Trent, you are two and a half years old this month!" I don't understand what he means, so I ask him, "I understand about birthdays, but why is this time significant?" He hesitates but then confesses, "I was at your exact age when my disease was first diagnosed. It changed my life, not so much at the beginning, but as my cancer treatments progressed, they took a toll on me. I went from being full of energy and mischief to being lethargic and docile. I lost weight, hair, and what my mommy called the sparkle in my eyes.

"The worst, though, was the way those close to us and even strangers no longer looked at me and smiled. Instead, they nervously stood in front of me and looked solemnly everywhere but at me. I wanted to cry out, 'I'm here, I'm here.'"

I feel bad for my angel. I now realize that even angels carry memories of life's scars with them. I ask him, "Why is it that an angel would be burdened with unpleasant memories of his time as a being of earth?" He quickly answers, "These memories are not a burden to me. It's necessary that I retain all experiences of life, good and bad, because they give me the wisdom necessary to guide you through your life. They provide the bearings of life's compass: morality, ethics, justice, generosity, compassion, kindness, trustworthiness, honor, loyalty, faith, reverence, and so much more. An angel can't become a guardian angel without experiencing life first." I ask him, "What was your name as a being of earth?" And his reply: "The same as it is as a spirit of heaven."

8

HAPPINESS INSPIRES HOPE

In June the summer heat rapidly returns, limiting my outdoor time once again to predawn and early morning runs with Mommy and early evenings with her and my kids. I continue to have stomach pain after feedings and spit up as usual. The critical three pounds I lost while battling my pneumonia and respiratory infections through the winter and spring are very difficult to gain back, given my eating abnormalities.

When people see my kids, I hear them say, "Look how big they're getting" or "They're growing like weeds." When they see me, all they can say is "Look how long he's getting!" That's it. My angel replies, "That's better than saying, 'He looks like a string bean,'" and then he chuckles. What they see and say probably depends on which side of me they're looking at. Because of the more frequent fractures in my left leg, it's stunted and about two and a half inches shorter than my right leg. "It's okay," my angel informs me. "When I was a little being of earth, I saw a Christmas movie about a boy called Tiny Tim, who also had a stunted leg. Everyone loved him, just like everyone loves you." My angel always knows how to make me feel better.

One day toward mid-June Mommy and Daddy announce that someone is moving in with us. I have a terrible fear it might be another animal or something like that. The kids immediately start being silly and throw out names ranging from friends and cousins to movie characters. Mommy says, "This girl will help take care of Trent and watch you kids whenever needed." I think, If only I could talk I would yell out, "PLEASE LET IT BE AUNT BEC!" When Mommy gleefully declares, "It's AUNT BEC!," the kids loudly celebrate the news. The girls immediately beg Mommy to put her in their room, but Mommy says, "I don't think so. Aunt Bec will stay in the extra upstairs bedroom. And to make her feel loved, we will need to respect her privacy and be quiet at night." I think to myself, My kids be quiet? Good luck with that! Aunt Bec moving in to be with me is my best blessing ever. My angel helps me channel a prayer of gratitude to God for this special gift He has given me.

Once Aunt Bec settles in, she spends most of her spare time with me and my kids and her Buddy. Last year she bought a horse named Buddy that was specially trained to provide therapy for physically disabled and mentally challenged children. Initially, she and Mommy hoped that Buddy's talents might one day help me, but my physical and mental difficulties exceed Buddy's capabilities.

My angel tells me that Mommy's and Aunt Bec's birthdays are this week: Aunt Bec's on July 2 and Mommy's on July 4, which is also the birthday of our nation. He says, "That special day is a national holiday filled with traditional celebrations like parades, family picnics and get-togethers, and patriotism. Throughout the nation, it culminates in a glorious fireworks display after dusk." On the evening of the 4th we celebrate Aunt Bec's and Mommy's birthdays, singing both the birthday and the "Sto lat" songs. Later, while my family goes to watch the fireworks, I stay at home with my Aunt Bec, who cuddles with me on the front swing while we listen to the distant booms of celebration.

As summer continues, Aunt Cathy and Uncle Eric ask family members for prayers and counseling as they consider adopting two children, a sister and brother, currently in the foster-care program. Ev'e, who is two and a half, and Masonn, who is one, come from a very abusive background and must be adopted together. Each has severe emotional pain and distrust issues to overcome, and Masonn faces years of physical, behavioral, and speech therapy. Aunt Cathy and Uncle Eric, who have five children and home school them, were approached by the foster-child agency as a preferential match with preapproval for the adoption. My aunt and uncle leave the matter in God's hands and make an appointment to meet and spend time with Ev'e and Masonn. I pray that these two children who need love and care will join our family.

A representative of our hospice service calls Mommy today and tells her that their office submitted my name as a possible recipient to the Wish With Wings charity. She happily informs Mommy that I have been chosen to receive a weeklong, all-expenses-paid, family trip to Give Kids The World in Orlando, Florida. That evening when Daddy gets home from work, Mommy excitedly shares the news with the family and Aunt Bec. Initially, everyone is stunned, speechless, and awed. God works in wondrous ways, for we are being sent to the very place our mud-run donations have helped other families to enjoy. Once Mommy's news sinks in, the family gives thanks and reverence to the Lord, who is doing such wonderful things for us. When Mommy tells us we will go in September and Aunt Bec will come with us, my heart leaps up. That's the news I want to hear!

Aunt Cathy and Uncle Eric, after much thoughtful prayer, announce to our families that they have moved Ev'e and Masonn into their home. After the required six-month waiting period, the children will be adopted into their family and our extended families. I give prayerful thanks to God for my aunt and uncle and for my soon-to-be new cousins.

When we meet these new cousins, Ev'e seems shy and quiet. In her short life, she has suffered multiple bone fractures and only God knows what else from those who were supposed to care for her. Masonn looks away from anyone who approaches him, and his basic communication skills and physical abilities are limited. During the first year of his life, he was strapped into a car seat day and night and only removed to change his diapers and clothes. The captive restraints have affected his physical development and actually deformed and flattened the back quarter of his skull. My angel describes their lives being saved by Aunt Cathy and Uncle Eric as an act of divine intervention.

My kids have been patiently counting down the days till our departure. Today is the day we will fly to Orlando and arrive at Give Kids The World later this afternoon. My angel is as excited as my family. Daddy is busy gathering the luggage, all my medications, medical records, and anything else we might need and staging everything at the front door. A Wish With Wings is providing a breathing machine, a feeding pump, and bulk diapers and wipes for me, saving Mommy and Daddy from having to transport all that equipment. It's a huge relief for them. A Wish With Wings also said they would furnish us with a ride to the airport. My family is totally floored when a huge car, called a stretch limousine, pulls up to our house to pick us up! This extravagance turns out to be a preview of how the generosity and care of this organization will exceed our expectations in absolutely every way throughout the trip.

    The kids have lots of questions while Mommy, Daddy, and Aunt Bec try to coax them to pose for pictures in and around the limo. Once the driver finishes loading the luggage in the trunk, helps us get situated in the limo, and starts heading to the airport, he asks my kids where they are flying to. All three answer simultaneously in a bombardment of explanations. The driver nods his head attentively to their excited answers the whole way to the airport. As he pulls up to our terminal and unloads the luggage, he simply says, "I can't wait to hear more when you return!"

    Rachel, our Wish With Wings coordinator, meets us outside the terminal with a bag of goodies for the plane ride and games for the trip. She tries get us help with our luggage, but Mommy says it isn't necessary and that we can manage. Rachel then insists on getting the kids some snacks at the gift shop and hands Mommy and Daddy an envelope containing a generous amount of money. It will prove to be enough to cover gas for the rental van they furnish us with while we are in Florida, our meals in the parks, Mommy and Daddy's date night out, and souvenirs for each of my kids at each of the parks. At the end, Mommy and Daddy still have money left over to return to them.

    When we arrive at the gate, Rachel ushers us onto the plane to ensure that we are comfortably settled in the seating she arranged, the first row of the coach section. Here there is extra room for my family to stretch out, for my kids to enjoy their goodies and games, and for me to get passed around. Her personal attention to all that we need, even if we don't know we need it, is much appreciated.

With the crew attentive and no delays, the plane ride is easy. My kids become engrossed in one of their new games, which makes the time fly for them. While Aunt Bec feeds me a bottle, my angel tells me about all the theme park attractions he is looking forward to seeing. When he finishes talking and I finish both the bottle and spitting up, I fall asleep listening to my Scout's musical selection.

I wake up as we start to deplane, and my angel explains the scene to me. Displayed throughout the terminal are all the area theme park "decorations," which is what my kids excitedly call the advertisements. Their heads keep turning all around to see these ads as Mommy and Daddy usher our family through the long corridors to the rental van waiting for us. Finally, an hour later we drive through the entrance to Give Kids The World.

Pulling up to the reception building, the House of Hearts, we are greeted by a big bunny rabbit named Mayor Clayton, who is actually the mayor of the resort. He escorts us inside where more people greet us and lead Mommy and Daddy to the registration area.

Meanwhile, Aunt Bec takes us kids to explore the area, and as we turn a corner, everyone spots a very important building: the Ice Cream Palace. Mommy told my kids earlier that they serve ice cream there for breakfast and all the rest of the day for free!

After we rejoin Mommy and Daddy, the reception people drive us to our villa in courtesy carts. On the way, we tour the streets and pass various resort attractions that the drivers describe to us. We pass so many villas, all colorfully painted in bright, festive colors, that my angel loses count. As the drivers circle around, they pull up to our villa, which faces a pond and a park in the center of which is Matthew's Boundless Playground, a happy attraction of this place. My angel describes our villa as bright yellow with white trim, with a plaque out front saying "Paces" and the house number 234. This is our happy home for a week. The attendants usher us in and tell us, "You are invited to attend Mayor Clayton's birthday celebration this evening and party with the other guests."

Mommy and Daddy take us kids and Aunt Bec to the festive birthday party where they serve cake and ice cream. We meet Mayor Clayton again, along with other Wish With Wings families. Aunt Bec signs up to volunteer her help at various resort attractions that we're visiting tomorrow. It's a wonderful start to a fabulous week!

The next morning starts with my kids going to have their ice-cream breakfast. Afterward, we set out to visit the resort's attractions. Our first stop is the Castle of Miracles, where my kids discover what it was like to be a prince or a princess during medieval times. I am honored with the gift of a special gold star that my kids decorate and give to the Star Fairy, who then takes the star and places it along with all the other Wish With Wings kids' stars on the domed ceiling. My star and all the other stars will remain there forever.

After spending some time at Keaton's Korral, the resort's stable where the kids ride horses, we have lunch at the Gingerbread Restaurant, a full-size gingerbread house inside and out. After lunch we are surprised with a personal visit by Mickey Mouse! He comes to meet me and spend time with all of us. Before leaving, he gives me a small Mickey Mouse doll and signs it. We then spend the rest of the afternoon at the huge pool and water fountains in the Park of Dreams. I sleep comfortably in my stroller.

The next morning my kids enjoy their ice-cream breakfast while Mommy feeds and dresses me. When they return, we all jump in the van and head to SeaWorld. My angel is as excited as my kids.

With all its outdoor attractions and interactions with sea life, SeaWorld is amazing! We could pet some marine animals, feed them, and even swim among some. There are awesome underground tanks with windows in their sides and floors that allow us to view the marine life from all around. It is cool and pleasant there, and the lighting is low. My angel fills my mind with the sights my kids are viewing. There are also cool amusement rides, interactive games, and live sea-life shows that get us wet and make us laugh. Our time there flies by, and all too soon we have to leave.

When we return to the resort, Daddy takes my kids to Marc's DinoPutt Golf Center. Thick with jungle everywhere, it has dinosaur obstacles and hidden dinosaurs that spring out at you throughout the course. When you sink the ball in the hole, it springs right back out. All my kids beat Daddy.

That night Mommy and Daddy go to Disney's Epcot Center for a date night. After Aunt Bec cooks my kids a meal at the villa, they are escorted by village staff to the resort's evening entertainment, "Village Idol," where they perform as contestants and enjoy some time with the other guest kids. Aunt Bec spends the evening in with me.

The next day, Aunt Bec is up early and, while everyone else sleeps, takes me and my angel for a stroller ride in the cool, early morning air. Out of nowhere I start my loud belly laugh, for the first time without my angel's help. Aunt Bec stops the stroller and starts laughing, too. People passing by us slow down for a look and start to chuckle and laugh. Still others farther away smile and wave. For no particular reason this time becomes the happiest of my life. My spontaneous laughter turns out not to be an isolated incident; that week I break out into belly laughs several times. My angel is happy that I have found an island of serenity and peace this week.

My family finally rolls out of bed and prepares for the new day. The kids skip the ice-cream palace so they can get to Universal Studios sooner. On the way there in the van, my kids rattle off all the attractions they want to see or do. I am only able to ride a train and do an interactive maze in Seussland. At Jurassic Park I hang out with Aunt Bec in the research center. Even though I don't understand a lot of what Aunt Bec is telling me about the center, I enjoy it because it is air conditioned. The rest of the family and my angel are busy checking the things they want to do and see in the park off their lists.

When the family rejoins us, there is no stopping the kids' excitement and stories of their amazing day. That night we eat in and watch them reenact their adventures in the Wizarding World of Harry Potter, Dr. Seuss Landing, and Jurassic Park. Clearly exhausted, the kids all go to bed early.

This morning Mommy takes me jogging while Daddy gets the kids going. He and Aunt Bec then accompany them to the Ice Cream Palace for breakfast. We all reunite at the villa to prepare for today's activities at the resort. First, we explore Matthew's Boundless Playground, home of the world's largest life-size Candy Land board game. The kids and adults play on the game board for the remainder of the morning. Then we eat lunch back at the Gingerbread House and meet more Disney characters. My angel says one is Goofy and another is Belle. The Belle person is a girl, and she spends a lot of time with me. I do so love Give Kids The World!

A little later rain clouds start to gather, so we take the van to visit the Amberville Train Station, a large and cool (according to Mommy and Daddy) retro game room. It has video games, board games, books, old TV programs, and interactive games from long ago when they were kids. It's enough to entertain my family through the rain storm and more.

Tonight the resort is hosting a summer Christmas party for all the Wish With Wings kids and their families. When we arrive, we are greeted by more Disney characters and other magical creatures and are directed to the main hall. My angel says, "Wow. It's decorated just like at Christmas time, complete with Santa sitting in a big red chair. And there is a Christmas tree with gifts under it! I wonder who they are for?" Christmas music is playing, and pixies and fairies are dancing to the music. Other characters are mixing with the guests, directing some to Santa for pictures. Later we discover who the gifts are for: a special gift is given to all of the Wish With Wings kids and their brothers and sisters, too. Treats are plentiful, and, of course, ice cream is everywhere.

The next morning is filled with the excitement of going to Disney World. We enter the park early with other Wish With Wings families and are given special passes to avoid long lines later in the day. My kids and my angel go on rides called Space Mountain, The Haunted House, Splash Mountain, and more. I join the whole family on rides through Buzz Lightyear's Adventure and It's A Small World (my favorite). Mommy, Daddy, and Aunt Bec take turns carrying me through the Swiss Family Treehouse. We visit the Hall of Presidents, where it is cool and dimly lit, but I don't understand much of what Mr. Lincoln says.

Unfortunately, I experience a diaper blowout there. My tummy blockage suddenly lets loose, and I do mean loose. Mommy is holding me, so the explosion destroys her shirt and shorts and mine, too. When we leave the theater, Mommy is certain our clothes are too soiled to clean up here and let us to stay for tonight's parade. Fortunately, an attentive Disney employee, who sees our dilemma, walks over to ask how she can help and, hearing Mommy's explanation, calls her supervisor. Once he understands the problem, he assures us we will be taken care of and leads me and Mommy through a back corridor to a store, where they provide both of us with new Disney shirts and shorts and won't accept any payment for them. My angel says this is yet another example of the kind and caring people here and throughout our trip that go out of their way to make sure this vacation is worry-free.

The parade has lots of very good music that I enjoy with my kids and my parents. When I discover that the parade will end with a gigantic thunderboom display, I am a little anxious. They call it "fireworks," but it's very much louder than the fireworks that Aunt Bec and I listened to in July. My angel understands that the loud noises frighten me, so he covers my ears throughout the show and I hear only silence. When we get home, he sighs contentedly, "This was one jam-packed day!"

Everyone sleeps in the next and final full day and night at Give Kids The World. After the ritual ice-cream breakfast, Mommy and Aunt Bec take the girls to the resort's salon, Twinkle Hope's La Ti Da Royal Spa. Daddy goes with Tyler and me to the resort's Happy Harbor Fishing Pond, where us guys enjoy a couple hours of fishing and exploring. When the girls join us later, we all go hiking on the back trails before lunch. Afterward, we spend the afternoon at the pool.

This evening is Pirate and Princess Night, and we are all entertained by pirate characters and princess dancers. My kids don pirate hats and, with all the other guest kids, join in the festivities. Some family friends from back home who recently moved to this area join us at the party, and later we all go for a night swim and ice cream.

It has been another wonderful day, ending an even greater weeklong retreat from the difficult realities of life. My family and all the others who enter the gates of Give Kids The World are so blessed to be honored and loved by all who make this experience not only possible but so special. Wish With Wings, the organization that brings kids like me and our families to places like this, gives our families, long after we are gone, lasting memories of what once was. [All the great things that Give Kids The World does and information on their programs and volunteering can be viewed at www.gktw.org. Programs and information about A Wish With Wings can be seen at www.awishwithwings.org.]

9

I AM A MIRACLE

It's good to be going back to Texas, but as our flight home starts, my tummy begins to hurt. My angel diverts my attention and makes the flight go faster by filling my mind with vivid scenes of our stay at Give Kids The World. It's a wondrous gift that adds a temporary window of sight to my memory of sounds, so I can bask in seeing my family.

    Fall soon returns, and we are spending the pleasant early evenings on the front swing. As the leaves fall from the trees, the family conversations turn to the upcoming third mud run. The event this year has been moved away from the Trinity River bottoms to a land preserve about thirty miles south of Fort Worth. Overall, there are fewer entrants, and the course is more primitive, which is exactly the way my team likes it. The day of the run they crawl and trudge through muddy trenches and jump over and into water-filled pits. They race between obstacles and on to the finish line where, triumphantly, they revel in their success. Victory does come at some painful cost though: spectator cousin Brady, who is one and a half, is bitten by something that causes his arm to swell to twice its size. Uncle Brandon, his daddy, is a fireman and paramedic and knows what to do; he takes him to the event paramedics and they fix him up. Cousin Matthew, who is three years old, steps into a fire-ant pile and receives several painful bites, but he's fine. They're a tough bunch!

The contributions we receive for A Wish With Wings total $3,000. God bless all for their generosity.

Now the Christmas season is here, and Mommy and my kids are busy preparing our home to celebrate the birth of our savior and welcome the Christ Child. My angel is excited and continues to share more memories of his childhood Christmases, which give us both much joy. Then it's my birthday again, and I discover something really wonderful about it. My angel explains to me that the Advent calendar starts on December first—my birthday—and progresses each day until Christmas. Each morning my kids excitedly open an Advent calendar door, revealing a special prayer, thought, or picture that they contemplate. It all starts on my special day and leads to the Baby Jesus' special day! I love to hear everyone sing "Sto lat" and the birthday song!

Christmas Eve is once again spent sharing family traditions first at Bapcia and Dzia Dzia's home and then at MiMi and Pop Pop's home. Mommy tells me of my beautiful Christmas stocking from Aunt Chris that will hang with our other stockings. Things are even more celebratory this year with the addition of Ev'e and Masonn to our family, bringing the total of grandchildren for Bapcia and Dzia Dzia to thirteen. We play, pray, eat, and open gifts together.

On Christmas day each family celebrates the birth of Jesus at its own home. Once again my angel leaves for the day to witness his own family's celebration. That morning I pray to God that when the time comes for me to go to my heavenly home, I may return each Christmas to witness my family's celebrations, just like my angel.

New Year's Eve arrives, and I and my family give thanks and praise to God for the many blessings bestowed upon us this past year: Hospice Service caring for me, cousin Marhia's adoption, HGTV's "Curb Appeal" remodeling our house and erecting my new swing, Aunt Bec moving in to help me and Mommy, the worry-free vacation gift to our family from A Wish With Wings and Give Kids The World, and Ev'e and Masonn joining our family. What a miraculous year!

In January, I notice something odd going on. My angel tells me, "Your mommy told your kids that you are going to start school." I answer, "Me?" He nods his head and replies, "Yes, you. Not at home like your kids' home schooling, but riding a special yellow school bus to a real school." The bus will take me to a Euless, Texas, school with a special needs education program that I will attend with four other kids. The bus will pick me up in my wheel chair at 7 a.m. and bring me home at 2 p.m. My teacher, Mrs. Thompson, must be really really really patient.

Mommy takes me the first few days of school and stays the first day to check out my teacher's and others' interactions with me. She is concerned about my feedings and the administration of my medication being timely. My therapists will come to the school for my weekly treatments. Once she is satisfied, Mommy allows the bus to pick me up and drop me off at home.

As this month ends and February begins, things are going well at school. My angel tells me that the other kids in my class are more capable of understanding and learning than I am. Even though the teachers know I can't do a lot, they still include me in the learning activities and storybook reading time. When I recognize a word they say, I flail my arms so they know that I am listening and understanding, but they think I'm doing it because I have gas or something. I do appreciate their efforts and kindness to me. My time at school also gives Mommy time to homeschool my kids and to do other things. I feel it's the least I can do for my mommy. My kids kiddingly say, "You are *so* lucky because you don't have any homework." Seriously? My schooling comes with a lot more pressure than they know!

Today, Ev'e and Masonn were officially adopted. Aunt Cathy told Mommy that Judge Geraldine Smith once again presided over the proceedings, and again she made the ceremony personal, special, and most memorable. I have witnessed many such people in my short life; they go way out of their way to make otherwise total strangers comfortable in their own skins, in their lives, actions, and current situations. Without motive or agenda, bias or prejudgment, they move beyond a personal comfort zone to reach out and positively touch or even alter the lives of their fellow human beings. In my case, what others see as a physical negative or hopelessness they turn into a positive inspiration.

My angel tells me that people aren't all the same. In my dark world I can only discern people by their voice tones. He says, "People are born either as men or women and can be many different colors: white, black, brown, yellow, olive, and mixtures of each. They live in different regions or countries and speak distinctly different languages. They can belong to many different religious faiths or hold naturalist beliefs or go to no church at all. This is what is called world diversity. Yet the one common thread is that they are all children of God." "Even the nonbelievers?" I ask. "Yes," he replies. How lucky we all are!

This year, my cousin Ashley joins brother Tyler and cousin Drew to compete in the cardboard boat regatta. Their newly constructed three-person boat is named

"Streaker" by the crew. They challenge all others in the youth Dolphin category and make it into the finals, where they capture first place. Congratulations to the crew!

My school is out for the summer, so I stay home now. The summer heat, once again, has driven me indoors for most of the day. But I still get to enjoy my morning run and early evening swing time with Mommy.

In July, we're on the road heading to Rockford, Illinois, for Great Bapcia's eighty-sixth birthday and to visit family. We'll stay again with Mommy's cousin Kristin and her husband Fred and their girls, Abby and Natalie. I'm looking forward to the cooler days ahead. Mommy brought the running stroller with us so we can go on morning runs in her cousin's neighborhood. Bapcia and Dzia Dzia are also in town for the week and are coming over for dinner, along with Dzia Dzia's sister Peg and brother Billy, their families, and most importantly Dzia Dzia's Aunt Barb.

It's a great evening to be out! Once all the families arrive, the kids start playing slow-pitch baseball. Uncle Billy offers to pitch to make the game fairer, but my angel says he seems to pitch slower to the girls. Aunt Barb sits next to Mommy and me and softly speaks to me about her great granddaughter. After dinner all the kids prepare for the main event: watching the fireflies ushering in the night sky.

Great Bapcia's birthday celebration is festive and full of laughter and love. She's a gentle and kind woman who revels daily in her blessings and her family. My angel tells me, "Your other great-grandparents are in heaven. On your mommy's side your great dzia dzia's name is Eddie, and your great-grandparents are named Bill and Fran. On your daddy's side, your great-grandparents are named Johnny and Marion and your great-grandfather's name is Lee." I have one more great-grandmother, Becky, who is still living.

The occasion is the perfect end to our summer trip. As we drive back to Texas, my angel tells me that my great-grandparents will be the first family members to greet me in heaven, along with my cousins Lucy, Christopher, and Aimee. For that I am truly grateful.

On our return home we are met with the tragic news that Kidd Kraddick suddenly died from a heart attack he suffered at a fund-raiser event for his charity foundation Kidd's Kids. He will be missed by the many families he benefited and by those he encouraged to give to others. I'm sure God will make him a "special guardian angel."

The fall season has arrived, with cooler temperatures and many activities. In October, my kids once again transform themselves into a pirate, a princess, and a chectah in order to go door to door in our neighborhood collecting their candy booty.

In November Mommy, Daddy, Tyler, and Triny participate in the Fort Worth annual Turkey Trot 5K run. Their successful completion garners generous donations to my Trent's Team fund. Along with money raised by an ice-cream sale fund raiser, Trent's Team is able to contribute $2,700 to A Wish With Wings this year. God bless everyone who helped make this a success.

My angel wakes me early this morning, announcing, "It's December first!" I start to say, "So wha–" but he interrupts and declares, "It's your fourth birthday, Trent! Tonight you're having a wonderful party with cake and ice cream." I have to admit that I fail to understand my angel's and fellow humans' focus on food, especially ice cream. My 80ml bottle every few hours is more than I can handle.

My family, aunts, uncles, and cousins celebrate my birthday at Bapcia and Dzia Dzia's home. Great Bapcia and Aunt Kiki are visiting from Illinois as well. They all sing the happy birthday and Sto lat songs to me. They make me a Yo Gaba Gaba cake, but I feed on their love tonight.

Soon after my birthday, an odd and extremely sharp pain begins, of course, in my tummy. Over the past year and a half, in addition to my normal tummy pain after eating and spitting up, I have developed bowel blockage, which results in the eventual exploding diaper phenomenon. I am guilty of exploding on just about everyone who has held me.

Now the pain is much more extreme, but the result is the same: a mess. Mommy takes me in to my doctor to determine what is causing the increased pain. My angel manages to cloak the most extreme spikes, and Mommy has determined that holding me in a folded fetal position with my head downward helps relieve some of the pain until I explode. My doctor concludes that a segment of my intestine is folding into itself or, as he puts it, telescoping and thus creating a recurring blockage. He explains that this condition can normally be relieved by an operation; however, given my frailty, it's out of the question.

Mommy meets with the Medically Dependent Children's Program of Medicare for my case review, updating them on my chronic respiratory care and now my daily bowel-restriction condition. The agency agrees to the need for daily full-time nursing care for me and approves payment for someone to provide it. As Mommy begins the interview process, a beautiful nurse-lady by the name of Angela arrives at our home to apply. She has ample experience, interacts well with me, and is very pleasant. My angel tells me the name "Angela" means angel, and that information totally sells me. Mommy offers Angela the position, and she accepts.

During this same time period I start to experience seizures brought on by noise stimulation from my Yo Gaba Gaba recording and some of the songs from my Scout stuffed toy. What a bummer! I love those toys.

In the meantime Miss Angela has proven to be very capable, helpful, and caring. Mommy and my kids are beginning to prepare our home for Christmas, and for me, it can't come quick enough. Although helpful, my pain-management medications, altered to help me tolerate the extreme pain from my bowel constriction, put me in a dazed state. So I am less conscious of my environment and regrettably of the magic and reverence of Christmas. My angel, though, is able to overcome my foggy state when talking with me, and he keeps me up to date on what's going on. Christmas seems to pass as if it were in slow motion. In that sense I am able to savor each sporadic conscious experience all the more.

Early in 2014, my angel begins filling my mind with past segments of my life in chronological order starting with the moment of my essential being. I've learned so much. From the start, I learned that God loved me and had a special plan for me. He provided me, a being of earth, with a spiritual guide in life. My guide, my angel, has taught me the meaning of life and God's life mission for me. He has brought light to my dark world. His counsel has helped me understand about the good and evil of humanity and about the salvation of the faithful through the miraculous birth of the Christ Child, His persecution, death, and resurrection.

With my angel's help and God's direction I have persevered through all the painful tests, biopsies, and traumas. Then and now, he cloaks my pain both physical and emotional.

I have lived to learn the joyous aspects of life. Among them, the most important have been the unconditional and everlasting love of my mother and the comforting, loving hands and voices that have made me part of a family. I have experienced the generosity of those who witnessed me and supported Trent's Team's and our charities. I have been the recipient of life-saving care from countless strangers in hospitals and clinics and critical care at home from Hospice service volunteers and medical professionals.

Countless prayers have been offered on my behalf, for which I am so very grateful, and I have been blessed to witness miracles of faith, hope, and charity. To my God, I thank you for my daily breath.

It's now early March, and my angel announces to me, "The time has come. I am now permitted to reveal my birth name to you." He says simply, "I'm Todd, and I'm happy to meet you, Trent." I am immediately overwhelmed with emotions of relief and resounding joy. I insert his name into the silly name game song he taught me, which triggers my uncontrollable exuberant belly laughter:

> Todd, Todd bo bod
>
> bo nana fana fo fod
>
> me my mo mod, Todd!

The whole night I continue to think of Todd's name and that song a lot. Aunt Bec is watching me, and I'm afraid my laughter is keeping her up a lot. She doesn't seem to mind, though, and laughs along, too.

My life seems to be coming full circle. My angel Todd is talking now more about my spiritual being and less about matters of my earthly being. I feel as though I'm at the cusp, the tipping point, of my life. It's actually quite calm and pleasant here and brings me clarity and allows me contemplation.

So after I have been meditating, I have only this one prayerful request, dear God:

When my time comes, please grant my family the strength to rejoice rather than grieve and to join me in celebrating my deliverance from my earthly constraints and my elevation to walk with Todd and the other angels in heaven. Amen.

APPENDIX

Trent's Poem

By Nicki, Trent's Mommy

It was apparent from your birth
Your time would not be long on earth.
How could such a blessing
So quickly become a curse?
It broke our hearts to see
That He made you differently.
We begged Him to fix you, to change you somehow,
To reveal a miracle right here and now.

The pain was unbearable, your future so bleak,
How could our God make this kind of mistake?
We tried everything to fix this and travelled to "the best,"
The one doctor to say that he could fix this mess.
Even the doctors could not find what was wrong

So we were left to let you grow and see what you would
    become.

Where is the God that would always be there,
The one who was faithful, gave us hope, and answered
    prayers?
Why have you left us when we are hurting so much?
More than ever we need to feel your touch.

The days became months and the months became years.
There was so much heartache and pain and tears,
But sometimes we would catch a glimpse of heaven in his
    laughter or his smile
And God didn't seem so far away after a while.

And then a voice spoke to us, from out of the blue,
"He is perfect to me. My eyes see more than you.
You are standing way too close to see the beauty of my way.
My master plan will be revealed for all to see one day.
In his short life he will touch people the way I need him to.
*My will is done through his hardships—it's a job I created him to
    do.*
I need him to plant a seed in some very special hearts.
So that my story may be revealed, he has to play this part.

You see his pain, you see him cry, you see his suffering,
But close your eyes and walk by faith and not by what you see.
You may not know the answers, and I understand your doubt;
Know, my child, that this is what faith is all about.

There are people who need a miracle to let Me in their lives.

I am letting you hold that miracle, but only for a while.
He does this job I gave him with such courage and such charm;
He does exactly what he needs to, and soon he'll be in my arms.
What you see as suffering is really grace, you know,
Revealed in a tiny package like so many years ago.
I know it hurts but I am holding you; you just have to trust in Me.
Take my hand; know that soon you will hold him for eternity.

I am the author of this story;
I wrote the beginning and the end.
I know this is a hard chapter for you to comprehend,
But if you just trust me and let me hold when you fall,
You will see there is a happy ending after all."

Now our perspective is changing and our eyes can see more
Than they were ever able to see before:
We see generosity in others because of this special little man,
And Jesus Himself is revealed to us time and time again.
Kindness and compassion from so many hearts,
Friends and family that lift us up through all the rocky parts.
We learn so much from just watching him live–
It is a struggle, but he has so much to give.
Slowly the sadness has been replaced by joy
And we see God's light daily through this amazing little boy.
And though he'll never walk or talk and we just live day by day
There is no limit to the people he will touch in his own special way.

The heartache remains and the tears still fall,
And sometimes the future looks grim.
But God will use our changed hearts in such a way
That will draw others closer to Him.

Lord, I can't say it in words....Can you just listen through my heart.

From Paulette

Trent,

You are such an amazing boy, truly a gift from God. You have been an incredible blessing to our whole family.

It has been so neat watching your mom and dad grow closer to The Lord and closer to each other over the last several years. Watching them care for you is such an example of Jesus' sacrificial love for us. It has been amazing to see you work in them. No matter how hard things get, they tirelessly care for you and rely on God's strength.

It has also been amazing to watch others gather around them and pour their love into you. Bapcia, Dzia Dzia, and Aunt Bec are incredible as they have dropped everything to help you and your family. They really enjoy spending time with you and love catching one of your smiles. They are an amazing picture of the body of Christ, and it has drawn our whole family so much closer together.

You have touched everyone in our family in so many ways. While your body is frail, you have an inner strength. You are a constant reminder that it is God who sustains us no matter what and a reminder of the frailty of life. We look forward to the coming kingdom, where our bodies will be made whole and we will run, skip, and laugh with you.

Uncle Eric and Aunt Cathy

My Dearest Trent,

On the day you were born, you opened the eyes and hearts of so many including me. Little did I know I was about to embark on a new journey that would touch my life and test my faith in so many ways.

Throughout the days and weeks following your birth I remember constantly searching for answers and scripture to hang on to just trying to understand what was going on. There you taught me Lesson #1: Trust in the Lord and keep searching and praying for answers. Even though the answers we were searching for never became known, I soon learned Lesson #2: We don't always get the answers we want; we get the answers that God wants us to have. After watching your family and Aunt Becca love you unconditionally until it hurts, adapting and welcoming your condition even with all of the unknowns, I saw them stronger than ever. They wanted to reach out and help other families like yours. They wanted to make it easier and happier by raising money not for themselves but for these families! Complete acts of unselfishness! Lesson #3: You have taught me to try to give unselfishly and to be thankful. Then through this last year when you have been in so much pain, and I can see the tears in your eyes and in the eyes of your family, you still manage to smile or laugh when the pain subsides. That is where I learned Lesson #4: Even through the pain and suffering there is good.

Trent, you inspire me to be a better person inside and out. You inspire me to be a better mom and to educate my children on the love, compassion, and prayers that we should have for those who might have a disability or that are different from us. You inspire me to share your story so that I might be able to help other families that go through these trials.

How is it that one little guy like you can make such a big impact on so many lives? God is GOOD!!! I thank God that you are here and that you have taught me many valuable lessons. You are an angel!

Love,

Aunt Katie

Trent's Story:

If people could hear me talk, they would hear me say, "Thank you, God, for letting me be born into the Pace family. You couldn't have picked a more loving and caring family for me." I would say thanks to my mom and dad and my three siblings for all the good and tough times we have gone through together, and I have a special place in my heart for Aunt Bec. There, I said it. Love, Trent

The Doyles

Since Trent's birth I have never been around a family so unwavering in their faith as the Paces are. I am so grateful to have witnessed that in my life time. When I went through a hard time early this year, I thought of Nicki and Shane and said to myself, They have such faith; I need that as well right now. I knew they had faith, but man they have blown my mind since Trent's birth. Trent has shown people that God has a bigger plan, and therefore we all need to allow it to happen. Trent has also shown me a much softer side to Kris; he cried in front of me when we found out about Trent. Trent has brought out the best in people that I did not know was there. I guess he has a way about him. Trent is such a blessed soul and has brought so much joy and heartache, but the joy outweighs the heartache. I just think of the strength and faith the Paces have and wish I had more of what they all have.

Aunt Kacey

Trent,

It is my opinion that children are the closest adults will come to purity until we die. We come into this world pure and innocent, not knowing sin, injustice, pain, or evil. As we grow, we see the wonders the world has to offer, learn to love, learn to hate, rejoice in relationships, cry when we are disappointed, make mistakes and learn from them. We try to live a life in the example of Christ, doing the best that we can. When I look at Trent I see purity. I see invincibility to sin, injustice, and evil. I see a child who, just by being, brings joy to so many and defines unconditional love.

I love you little man.

Cousin Kelley

Trent has taught me not to take things for granted and appreciate everything I have. Children do not worry about things like money, pollution, war, etc. I try to take some of that and apply it to my life. I try not to get too concerned with how bad life can be. But instead I think of how good it is. I try to find the good in every situation. I have a very stressful job, but I do not get stressed out. Not because I do not take what I do seriously, but I know life is too short and precious to waste on such a wasteful emotion. I think of my family—children, nephews, nieces, brothers, in-laws, etc.—and it makes me happy. Thinking of the sparkle in Trent's eyes and his cute little smile makes the rest of the crap the world throws at me just melt away. Trent made me stronger and better equipped to take on the bad in the world. I have prayed and still pray for Trent. It is hard to bring me down, with Trent in my emotional corner. I'm not a very religious man, but I do pray and attend church on occasion. God sent us an Angel with broken wings, but He still sent us an Angel. Much love for my nephew Trent.

Uncle Kris

Hi there! I wanted to submit a little quote from a book Nicki gave me when Ashlyn was born and in the NICU, but I have had a hard time finding it from our move! But I used my resources and I think I found what I was looking for!

"I love you just the way you are, but I'm not finished with you yet." From the book "Hermie: A Common Caterpillar" by Max Lucado.

What a wonderful tribute! Can't wait to read it!!!

Kristi

Trent—He has touched our hearts with joy and deepened our souls with reflection, attitude, and compassion. Clearly a special gift from God. Like Jesus and many before him, his suffering is for a greater purpose. We are blessed to have him in our lives. The mere thought of him brings sunshine to our hearts. We are also blessed and thank God for the family whose care he is in on earth. They have realized his potential for spreading goodness and love. We have all gained immensely from this angel. You can be assured that Great Dzia Dzia is watching over Trent.

Great Bapcia and Kiki

Never have I seen someone communicate so much with so little. Watching Trent crane his neck to follow the sound of Nicki and Shane's voices, the way he follows the sound of his brother and sisters' laughter as they run through a room, the way he smiles his special smile for Aunt Bec and of course the way he lights up when he hears DJ Lance Rock. I know Trent can't tell us with words, but I know he knows how much he is loved and feels JOY—what a beautiful testament to his amazing family. I love you all so much.

Aunt Kristin

Thank you for putting this book together. What a great testimonial to the wonderful impact that Trent has had on so many lives.

As for our family, Trent has shown us the unbelievable power that a simple smile can have on people. He has shown us that God's blessings are in the simplest and most common human gestures. That a tremendous amount of love can be radiated with no words being spoken. The few times that I have been privileged to hold Trent have had an enormous impact on me. It was like holding a little angel. It is almost like he is our entire extended family's guardian angel. The experience reinforced our own faith and beliefs, showing us how truly precious and beautiful life is, how to live each day and each moment to our fullest, to appreciate those around us, to hug, kiss, and say " I love you" every day, and to give thanks for how much as a family we are so richly blessed.

May God bless you and your family always.

We love you,

*John, Camie, Connor
and Christian*

Trenton is pure sweetness. When he smiles, it makes you want to be the best person you can be—a person who is gentler, more kind and more loving—so that you can be worthy of his trust and love. He makes everyone smile.

Love, Aunt Lin

T is for Tender and oh so sweet

R is for Remarkable—a treasure so rare

E is for Enchanting—he shines and he sparkles

N is for Never-ending cuddles, hugs and silly smiles

T is for Treasured and loved by so many!

Joy and Jim Baughman

Trenton

Trenton, you know me. I can tell. I pray for you, by name, every day at Holy Mass.

I don't pray so much for you to be healed; I just pray for God's will for you. That's really the best prayer for anybody.

Somehow, through the many days—years—of prayer, I have a sense of what you are about.

You are the happiest person I know, and I know a lot of people.

You often wonder if your family knows just how much you love them. You also know—profoundly so—that you are loved.

Trenton is surprised that so many people are worried about him, feel sorry for him, think that he is missing out on life. He knows better. Trenton doesn't want anybody to worry about him. He is in good hands, God's Hands. In fact, it is Trenton who worries about us.

Trenton is what is called a "victim-soul." He makes reparation for the many sins of the world, including mine, yours.

Trenton accepts his role in life.

He wonders if you catch the subtle, so very subtle hints that he gives you about love—real love, not what most people think of as love. There is a big difference; Trenton can teach those who are willing to learn.

Trenton appreciates every little thing that you do for him; every moment of it. It is a sacrifice for you, and he knows it.

Trenton has been baptized, and he is pretty sure that he is not capable of personal sin. He knows that he is destined for Heaven. So what would a total healing do? Could it jeopardize the very GIFT he has been given?

Trenton is an evangelizer. Very much like Pope John Paul, toward the end of his life: he couldn't talk, could barely do anything, anything that most of us would understand as something worth doing. But what Trenton is doing—what John Paul did—is giving us a sermon on life. Are we humble enough to listen?

We say that Trenton is "special." We have no idea how true that is! Oh, how God loves this young boy! How blessed are his parents, his siblings, his grandparents, his relatives, his neighbors!

We won't fully understand or appreciate the gift that Trenton is until (or unless!) we get to Heaven. He knows that Heaven is home.

There are small things, so many small things—a look, a touch, a view out of a window—that give Trenton a joy deeper than we could receive from any of our overblown diversions.

Trenton is weak, yet strong. He is faithful. Trenton carries his cross every day. He knows that he never carries it alone. Perhaps he feels the presence of his Savior. And Trenton does feel the presence of his family. He knows. He accepts.

In a world (especially the United States in the 21st century) that prizes the superficially perfect, the superstars, the utilitarian and throws away the rest, Trenton has come as a reminder that that is not all there is. That what we think is good is not necessarily as good as it seems. We are distracted and seduced by the same old tricks and ploys by the same being who fooled our first parents.

Trenton is a rebuke to the modernist world that, like the ancient Spartans, only sees the surface. We act as though we never want to die, forgetting that, in fact, though we are mortal, we also have an immortal soul. Trenton reminds us daily, if we pause and pay attention, that what counts and what is of real and lasting value is way deeper than most of us realize. He comes to wake us up out of our hypnotic trance.

It is all too easy and obvious to dwell on the many things that Trenton cannot do. Some of the things that he cannot do are most important: he cannot deceive; he cannot give someone the cold shoulder; he cannot gossip; he cannot steal; he cannot say words that hurt. The key to the secret of Trenton is to discover that which he can do. What Trenton can do is teach us. Trenton accepts God's will in his life. He does not struggle. He does not complain. He does not rebel. He accepts. With joy. Like a sweet little lamb, with no guile. I think that there is probably nothing so pleasing to God than a human being whose will is totally accepting of God's will. "Thy will be done." Let us learn that from Trenton. And let us be at peace and accept, with all the hurt and disappointment, and pain, that there is a time coming, not so very long from now, where these things will be done with and we will meet our God and be judged. In that day, Trenton will stand tall as a true hero, a real superstar, and as one who has finished the race and won. Let us, each in his own way, follow Trenton's footsteps.

So let us follow in the footsteps of he who cannot walk. Let us listen to the words of he who cannot talk. For Trenton is on the right path. And Trenton has wisdom. He tells us to be not afraid. He will take you by the hand and lead you to the place of safety and joy.

Michael Jones

I knew Trent was a special child before he was born, but did not know how very special he was and how he would affect my life. As he grew, I looked for answers for his many problems and did not find them. After months and months of searching I found, not answers, but strength, strength to go forward, at the foot of the cross. We may never find answers for Trent's physical problems, but he is doing the job God created for him.

Trent has touched my heart and soul with a tenderness and compassion I did not imagine. I look at others, especially those needing help, with a different vision than before. Through his eyes, I see hope, patience, suffering, compassion and faithfulness. He has touched so many lives—his smile lights up my heart, and cradling him gives me a special peace. He is my special little guy who has taught me so much about love and life without speaking. Love you little buddy!

Your devoted Bapcia

I was thinking of Trenton this morning, and it occurred to me how blessed we are that he is touching our lives. He has given so many people the opportunity to be generous with their hearts and money. He has changed people's perspectives on life and how to live it. He has brought people closer to God. He has brought families closer. That little angel has done an enormous amount of work. I read a prayerbook from Padre Pio, and he says on prayer: "Pray with perseverance, trust and a serene and calm mind, Pray, hope and don't worry, worry is useless. God is merciful and will hear your prayer. Prayer is the best weapon we have, it is the key that opens God's heart." Our lives and Trent's are in the palm of God's hands if we accept that. Trent is in very good shape with God because he is an angel sent to us from God, but we all have a little more work to do.... My dear friends, do not have fear for Trenton. He is doing the work he was sent to do. You are extremely strong and will guide your family through the rough waters. When you need it, you will have it.

Catherine

To say that Trent is a special little boy who has touched our hearts would be an understatement at best. His strength to fight and his courage to look fear in the face daily are an inspiration to us and have been for the last four and a half years. His trials and tribulations make ours seem very small and insignificant.

While we are not good at expressing our thoughts and heartfelt feelings and sharing them in print, we still wanted to be a part of this beautiful tribute to

Trent. So we have taken an excerpt from a poem and are sending it with much love to Trent, from his Pop Pop and MiMi.

Our Wishes for You

May you find serenity and tranquility
in a world you may not always understand.

May the pain you have known
and the conflict you have experienced
give you the strength to go through life
facing each new situation with courage and hope.
Always know that there are those
whose love and understanding will always be there,
even when you feel most alone.

May a kind word,
a reassuring touch,
and a warm smile
be yours every day of your life,
and may you give these gifts
as well as receive them….

May you always feel loved.
[from "May You Find Serenity" by Sandra Sturtz Hauss]

Dear Trent,

You are the little child that Christ urges us all to become so that we can run freely into his embrace. Your laughter is the pure joy of being loved by God, who cares for you so much that he has chosen you to share in his most intimate sufferings. You have become one with his Holy Heart, a vocation that requires such patience, such openness, and such courage that most of us fall very, very short of that intimacy with God. You are a blessing on us all. When I hear your laughter, I recognize in it the same joyfulness that your namesake, King David, expressed when he danced with abandon and ecstasy before the Holy of Holies and let his heart sing out:

> O God, you are my God—
> > for you I long!
> For you my body yearns;
> > for you my soul thirsts,
> Like a land parched, lifeless,
> > and without water.
> So I look to you in the sanctuary
> > to see your power and glory.
> For your love is better than life;
> > my lips offer you worship!
> I will bless you as long as I live;
> > I will lift up my hands, calling on your name.
> My soul shall savor the rich banquet of praise,
> > with joyous lips my mouth shall honor you!
> > > *Psalm 63:1-6*

The only thing better than life itself is God's love, which he has given you in abundance. You are rich in all that really matters: your own virtues—love, joy, patience, endurance, acceptance, wonder, and the Lord's peace that surpasses all understanding—and the love, compassion, and respect of your whole family. May you continue to teach us love and wisdom, long after the Lord embraces you and tells you, "You have done well, my child."

Aunt Chris and Uncle Bainard

I think of you now in awe as I pray,
God used such a little life in such a big way.
Through you so many saw their faith grow,
As we felt God hold us through the high and the low.
You taught us to smile through pain's deepest sting,
And join in the laughter when we hear its sweet ring.
The worries of this life that once seemed so key,
Melted away as we discovered life's not about me.
You inspired a movement—a mud-covered team,
And helped other families live one final dream.
We learned finding the answers wasn't the way;
It's about loving each other and giving all we can each day.

All that you taught us will stay in our hearts,
Your footprints will mend the most broken parts.
You strengthened our family, our faith and our joy,
All our lives altered by one little boy.
God gave you a job, just like the rest,
He knew our sweet Trent could teach us all best.

Aunt Bec